"This is a comprehensive and compelling read on how to make metaphors work in therapy. It is a light and interesting book that highlights the power and potential complexity of metaphor when harnessed appropriately by the therapist. It covers the scientific underpinnings of how metaphors work, and explains the best way to create a therapeutic context that will enable metaphors to do what they do best: create psychological flexibility in the way in which we relate to ourselves. The work is scholarly and timely, but it is also alive with interesting transcript segments and relevant clinical metaphors. The book is neither dumbed down nor hard to read. In fact, it was pleasurable and interesting, and takes the reader on a journey that will positively change the way therapists use metaphor in their clinical practice."

—**Yvonne Barnes-Holmes, PhD**, associate professor in behavior analysis at Ghent University

"If you have been craving a sophisticated and thorough discourse on all things metaphor, *Metaphor in Practice* is the book you need. Niklas Törneke provides a fresh, in-depth analysis of both the scientific role and practical application of metaphors in psychotherapy."

—**Jill A. Stoddard, PhD**, coauthor of *The Big Book of ACT Metaphors*

"This outstanding volume examines the use of metaphors in clinical practice. Although many experienced and skilled clinicians often use metaphors quite naturally, few therapists know why they use them and how they can maximize their benefits. This book systematically analyzes the theoretical foundations and optimal use of these powerful tools. Grounded in solid clinical science, metaphors provide therapists with a language to effectively communicate important clinical information that can have a powerful impact on the therapeutic process. I highly recommend this book."

—**Stefan G. Hofmann, PhD**, professor of psychology in the department of psychological and brain sciences at Boston University

"I have learned so much from this valuable book. Niklas Törneke demonstrates the beautiful synergy between therapeutic and linguistic analysis, and the outcome is both a practical guide and intellectual inspiration for practitioners, researchers, and everyone else interested in therapy and language."

—**Dennis Tay, PhD**, assistant professor in the department of English at the Hong Kong Polytechnic University

"In *Metaphor in Practice*, Niklas Törneke takes you on a journey that is both intellectually stimulating and incredibly practical. In the first part of the book, he shows the reader how metaphor is central to all aspects of therapeutic work, and provides the reader with an analysis of metaphor that is based on his deep understanding of philosophy, theory, and science. Then, in the second part of the book, he provides a stunning breadth of ways to create metaphors to help clients understand how they are influenced by their environment, get a healthy perspective on their experience, and find a valued direction for their life. The reader will find the chapter on cocreating metaphor especially useful, as it shows you how to move beyond canned metaphors and work cooperatively within the client's unique history and worldview. Törneke writes with clarity and beauty. I cannot recommend this book enough. It will be useful to anybody who seeks to use language to improve the human condition."

—**Joseph Ciarrochi, PhD**, coauthor *Get Out of Your Mind and Into Your Life for Teens*, and coeditor of *Mindfulness, Acceptance, and Positive Psychology*

METAPHOR
in
PRACTICE

A Professional's Guide
to Using the
Science of Language
in Psychotherapy

NIKLAS TÖRNEKE, MD

CONTEXT PRESS
An Imprint of New Harbinger Publications, Inc.

Publisher's Note

This publication is designed to provide accurate and authoritative information in regard to the subject matter covered. It is sold with the understanding that the publisher is not engaged in rendering psychological, financial, legal, or other professional services. If expert assistance or counseling is needed, the services of a competent professional should be sought.

Distributed in Canada by Raincoast Books

Copyright © 2017 by Niklas Törneke
                Context Press
                An imprint of New Harbinger Publications, Inc.
                5674 Shattuck Avenue
                Oakland, CA 94609
                www.newharbinger.com

Cover design by Amy Shoup

Acquired by Elizabeth Hollis Hansen

Edited by Susan LaCroix

Indexed by James Minkin

All Rights Reserved

Library of Congress Cataloging-in-Publication Data on file

19   18   17

10   9   8   7   6   5   4   3   2   1   First Printing

To Birgitta, Viktor, Ulrika, Hanna Klara, and the growing family.

Contents

Practical Scientific Knowledge About the Most Important Therapeutic Tool We Have

Imagine a plumber without tools.

When called in on a job, a plumber in this situation could do only a few simple things. Turn on or off a faucet. Pull a spoon out of the garbage disposal. Things like that. A task of any complexity would be impossible.

Psychotherapists without metaphors are like plumbers without tools. It is almost impossible to express complex ideas without relying on metaphor—which is why I'm beginning this foreword with one. Almost every sentence we speak includes obvious metaphors buried in the etymology and connotations of the words we choose, if not more obviously in our verbal constructions, such as the one I just gave. Our arguments and discussions are embodied in metaphor even in our physical postures and mental purposes, as we "run from" emotions that after all are hardly "chasing" us, or we "deal with" thoughts that are unable to negotiate. "Psychopathology" itself is a metaphor.

But while we need metaphor as applied workers, and we see metaphor in our clients and use them in almost every act we take in that role, it does not mean that we *understand* what we are doing. In the main, we do not.

The tools of psychotherapy are dominantly verbal, but that very fact is a problem. We all have an intuitive understanding of human language because we have been speaking and listening our whole lives, but that comfortable knowledge is the illusion of common sense.

This is easy to test. Ask a normal clinician the simplest question about human language and any pretense of scientific understanding will be revealed as illusion, like a curtain being pulled away from the Wizard of Oz. While prohibiting examples as substitutes for explanations (examples as substitutes for analytic knowledge is a certain route to self-deception), ask a clinician for a technical account of what a "word" is, or what verbal problem solving entails, or why metaphors are useful. The curtail will slide quickly to the side. You will encounter a mix of long pauses and vague common sense discussions. You will encounter the humbug of our commonsense understanding of how language and higher human cognition actually works.

One could be critical of therapists' dalliance with this level of ignorance, but in the main, scientific theories in this domain are far removed from the needs of practitioners. In the main, it is just not very useful for clinicians to read the scientific literature on metaphor, which has so very little to say that is powerful, tested, and known to be of practical importance. There is a vast body of work in mainstream science alright, but it is largely focused on the wrong things for the gritty work of behavior change. It leaves practitioners in a position like our proverbial plumber, who thinks to ask about how these tools work only to receive a complex and irrelevant treatise on their chemical composition.

Therapists need both. We need our verbal tools AND we need the kind of scientific knowledge that empowers their effective use.

Fortunately, that is not an impossible demand. Indeed, delivering on that agenda is what this book is about.

Niklas Törneke is a most unusual private practitioner. A Swedish psychiatrist, he has spent many years seeking out that combination of basic scientific principles and practical applications. He's shown the result of that journey with his excellent books on behavioral principles (Ramnerö & Törneke, 2008), and learning relational frame theory (Törneke, 2010). He has the kind of mind that keeps asking "why" and who refuses to stop reading and asking that question until the curtain of commonsense ignorance parts and he has an understanding that is both scientifically solid and clinically useful. Then he works hard to give away the knowledge he has unearthed, using clear language and careful explication. As a result, Niklas is in demand around the world as a trainer, speaker, and writer. He is not out there doing charismatic and flashy presentations on wild and untested clinical interventions: he is walking clinicians through his consolidation and analysis of complex scientific literatures, and the practical importance of these, in a calm, practically focused, step-by-step way. An intelligent, balanced, kind-hearted man, with a backlog of clinical experience and wisdom, his voice comes through clearly in this volume.

The book is structured as I would expect, knowing Niklas—it is structured the way he thinks. It begins with a question, and then carefully explores what is known. The search is thorough but not aimless since he has a practical purpose in mind and shares it with the reader. He settles on the aspects of the existing science that seem most useful—centering in especially on relational frame theory (RFT) and the body of work it contains on metaphor. Never doctrinaire, useful insights that are learned along the way are retained regardless of where they come from, RFT or not. Then with this understanding brought to the fore, he walks into common clinical tasks, and applies the science of human language and cognition to the interventions practitioners can make using metaphor to get the job done, showing in well-crafted dialogues how that knowledge applies.

This is not a book to be skimmed, or read by looking up terms in the index. This is a book to be read from front to back. I picture reading it the way it was likely written: thoughtfully, sitting is a comfortable chair, in a cozy office, with a cup of coffee and warm walls to defend from the cold outside. An honorable and interesting journey, crafted by an honorable and interesting man, for an honorable and interesting purpose: helping to change human lives.

Psychotherapy is a dominantly verbal interaction, and thus the tools of psychotherapy are dominantly verbal. We need to know what they are, and how they work. This book is about one of the most important and versatile verbal tools we have: metaphor. If there ever was a tool worthy of careful consideration in a comfortable chair in a cozy office, this is it.

Grab your coffee and have a seat.

—Steven C. Hayes
Foundation Professor of Psychology
University of Nevada

INTRODUCTION

A Tale of Three Books

Poetic imagery was an early element in my life. Swedish Nobel Laureate Pär Lagerkvist and other Swedish poets were frequently quoted in my childhood home while I was growing up, along with the biblical stories and their multi-layered narratives: "the Lord is my shepherd"; "The kingdom of heaven is like leaven…"; "You are the salt of the earth…"

Many years later (1993–1996) I trained as a psychotherapist. My classmates were a creative group and the environment was stimulating, albeit sometimes a little chaotic. I especially remember the discussions I had with one of them who was also a trained art therapist. I was fascinated by the way she interacted with her clients using drawings and art. Although the specific practicalities of this method were alien to me, in our dialogues it struck me that I could do the same using metaphor: I realized you could paint with words!

Another person who inspired me in the direction that led to this book was the cognitive therapist Art Freeman. As one of the teachers in the training program, he described a way of conceptualizing a psychological problem that appealed to me. After listening to a client's account he would make a simple drawing, often using stick figures, which summarized what he had heard as he saw it. Then he would hand the drawing to the client and wait for a response. In the dialogue that followed, the client would be encouraged to alter or correct the drawing to make it reflect her own perception of the situation. The two of them would then use the picture to work out what had to change. And again I realized: this can also be done using metaphor.

In 1998 I became acquainted with acceptance and commitment therapy (ACT), a treatment model that sets metaphor at the center of psychotherapy. I think it was at that time I first had the idea of writing a book on metaphor use. But other important things intervened. A year later I met Jonas Ramnerö, and our dialogue on learning theory-based psychological treatment has been going on ever since. Jonas came up with the idea of cowriting a book, which eventually became *The ABCs of Human Behavior: Behavioral Principles for the Practicing Clinician* (Ramnerö & Törneke, 2008). Some of my ideas on how metaphors can be used in therapy are included in that book (chapter 10).

My interest in ACT eventually stretched to its theoretical foundation, relational frame theory (RFT). It was very liberating to finally meet a scientific theory of human language and cognition useful for both basic research and clinical application. A brief introduction to the theory was also included in *The ABCs of Human Behavior* (chapter 7), but that was not enough. The task of presenting RFT in a comprehensive and yet readable manner led to a new book, *Learning RFT* (Törneke, 2010). Since RFT provides a model for how metaphors work, the book contains a fairly detailed section on the subject (chapter 5).

So the challenge of metaphor and its use in psychological treatment has followed me through the years. But in this I am definitely not alone. Wherever you look within the world of psychotherapy, regardless of the specific treatment model, everybody seems to agree on the importance of metaphor as a therapeutic tool. This is so within cognitive behavior therapy (Muran & DiGiuseppe, 1990; Linehan, 1993; Stott, Mansell, Salkovskis, Lavender, & Cartwright-Hatton, 2010; Blenkiron, 2010), psychodynamic therapy (Katz, 2013; Rasmussen, 2002; Stine, 2005), systems therapy (Barker, 1985; Combs & Freedman, 1990, Legowski & Brownlee, 2001) and experiential therapies (Angus & Greenberg, 2011). A historically important influence in general is Milton Erickson (Rosen, 1982). Metaphor use is also central to a whole range of popular models of self-development and change which are considered outside the group of evidence-based methods and which often make strong claims as to how metaphors work (Battino, 2002; Lawley & Tomkins, 2000).

But what about the scientific foundation of all this? What do we who take pride in conducting scientifically-based psychological treatment have to support any claims about the importance of metaphor? What do we know about how metaphors work in psychological treatment? Are there any scientifically-based recommendations as to how such work should be conducted? This book is my attempt to provide some answers to these questions.

However, even though there is general consensus about the relevance of the field of metaphor, it is not so clear where such knowledge is to be found. If you stand in the evidence-based tradition of CBT (cognitive and behavioral therapies) you would welcome data demonstrating differences in, say, the use of metaphor and absence of such use, or ways of using metaphors, and treatment outcomes. Unfortunately, the amount of research targeting such issues is small and what research does exist rarely gives clear answers to the questions raised (McMullen, 2008).

At the same time as the different psychotherapeutic schools, despite their positive outlook on the therapeutic use of metaphors, have had trouble finding ways to scientifically assess this, there is no lack of scientific analysis of the phenomenon of metaphor in human experience in general. On the contrary, this is a very productive and growing interdisciplinary field, in which linguistics and cognitive sciences have leading roles. In fact, linguists have even started to take an interest in how metaphors are used in psychotherapy (Needham-Didsbury, 2014; Tay, 2013; 2014).

Behavior analysis has also started to make a novel contribution to this area in recent years. With a new understanding of human language and cognition based on relational frame theory, the phenomenon of metaphor is now more accessible to behavior analysis.[1] In this sense, this book is a natural continuation of my two previous works. In our introduction to clinical behavior analysis, Jonas Ramnerö and I made brief mention of metaphors as part of clinical intervention; the book on RFT and its clinical application included an analysis of metaphor use in more detail. And now, in this third book, I place metaphors and their function center stage. What do we know and what advice is it reasonable to give on how metaphors should be used as part of clinical practice?

The home arena of this book is the same as for the two previous ones: behavior analysis as a scientific project. But since it is other scientific disciplines that have devoted more research to the subject of metaphor, this is where I will start. Let me make it clear, however, that my account will be a selective one. Metaphor research is a large and diverse field of knowledge, and what follows is not a general introduction to it. Of course, I will strive to do justice to the material, but I approach the task with a particular personal intention: to use this knowledge in the service of a modern behavior analysis of metaphor use. And all this in such a way that renders it practical and clinically relevant.

---

1   See Törneke 2010 for definition.

The Disposition of the Book

The book begins with a chapter (chapter 1) that introduces the subject area and provides basic definitions, with a focus on scientific developments since the 1980s. Chapter 2 highlights the trends in research over the last ten years, based on the observation that these overlap to a high degree with the positions of behavior analysis. Chapter 3 presents the positions and the relatively limited contribution of traditional behavior analysis, mainly consisting of B. F. Skinner's way of analyzing metaphor. Chapter 4 is central, giving a brief general introduction to RFT and, above all, illustrating how the approach can analyze metaphor use. Chapter 5 goes through the existing research regarding metaphor use in psychotherapy and presents some cautious conclusions. The research-oriented part of the book ends with a short chapter summarizing the main points so far (chapter 6), the intention being to offer the theoretically disinterested reader a shortcut to the clinical part. It is thus possible to start reading from here and then go directly to the clinical chapters. It is my hope, of course, that in this case the reader will later be drawn back to the first chapters of the book, having familiarized himself with the book's clinical section.

The clinical part starts with a chapter (chapter 7) that tries to identify a few basic principles of psychological treatment. A few basic treatment strategies are formulated, which should also guide the use of metaphor. The five chapters that follow (chapters 8 through 12) are intended to describe different aspects of concrete use of metaphor in treatment. A chapter on metaphors and experiential exercises (chapter 13) ends the clinical section, and then a poet gives us a final word.

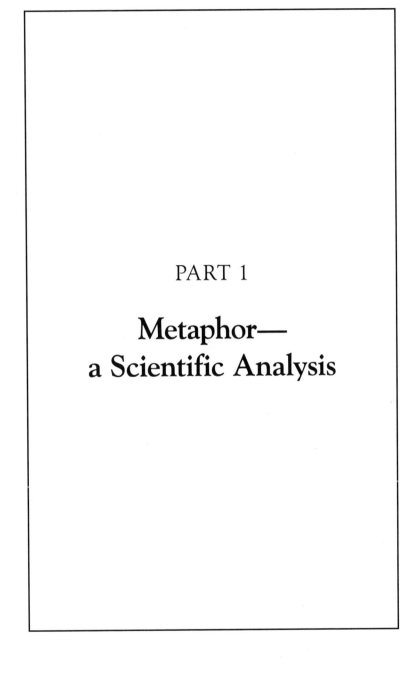

PART 1

Metaphor—
a Scientific Analysis

CHAPTER 1

What Are Metaphors?

I'm totally run down; everything's going downhill.

I'm just running round and round, like a hamster in a wheel, and I can't escape.

My head just won't stop buzzing. It's a wasps' nest in there!

I feel so empty; there is a huge hole inside.

Such figures of speech are frequently heard from clients describing their mental suffering—and, for that matter, from people in normal everyday conversation too. And it is extremely unlikely that anyone listening would actually believe that the speaker really is trapped in a giant exercise wheel normally designed for hamsters, or really does have a swarm of insects between her ears. We still often say things like this—and talk about one thing in terms of another. And it is by no means only people in some state of anguish who do so. In a counseling session, it is not uncommon for the therapist to use such modes of expression as well. In some forms of modern behavioral therapy, such as ACT (acceptance and commitment therapy), the therapist will make deliberate and systematic use of this way of communication. Thoughts, memories, and emotions are discussed as if they were passengers in a bus, desperate behavioral strategies are compared to digging deeper into a pit in order to get out of it, and a successful life strategy is described as "taking your keys with you" (Hayes, Strosahl, & Wilson, 2012).

Even therapists who work from models that do not particularly emphasize this type of linguistic convention use figurative language when, say, explaining psychological problems or therapeutic practices. A psychoanalyst talks of the "subconscious" and something called the "superego." So some phenomena that take place in a person's mind are described as being above (*super*) or below (*sub*) others. A cognitive therapist often describes the therapeutic relationship as "two scientists working together" (Beck & Weishaar, 1989, p. 30). In this, psychotherapists are only doing what people do in general—using one thing to talk about another. They use what we normally call metaphors. And even if there is reason for this type of language use to be more common in psychotherapy than in many other forms of dialogue (more on that later), metaphors are very common indeed. We say that the White House has said something when the US president makes a statement; we say that people who behave in an aloof manner are cold, and that those who greet us with understanding and friendliness are warm; brave people can be lionesses, and the fortunate might have won the jackpot despite not having used an actual slot machine.

The fact that metaphor use is a natural and universal part of human dialogue has occupied philosophers and scholars for centuries, and the question of how they operate and how they relate to language more generally is by no means new. A seminal analysis of this was done by Aristotle hundreds of years before the Common Era, and his writings on the subject still inform the debate to this day. In Aristotle's definition, "Metaphor consists in giving the thing a name that belongs to something else" (Aristotle, 1920, chapter 21, 1457b 1–30), arguing from the given assumption that a word has a "real" meaning and that metaphors (amongst other figures of speech) are a modification of the more genuine, "conventional" sense. This fundamental notion, that metaphors are a secondary linguistic function, has dominated our view of metaphors ever since. We see language as being basically "literal" and metaphors as being a particular development of this literality, a kind of specialist tool suited for artistic purposes, such as poetry or rhetorics. Alternative views have sometimes emerged, but have been largely ignored or forgotten.

Aristotle's philosophy of metaphor continued to reign supreme throughout much of the twentieth century. We might assume that it is bound up, at least in part, with empirical positivism and its influential status in epistemology (Billow, 1977; Ortony, 1993). In this view, words denote "facts" in the real, external world, and since someone who describes his stressed, tormented state is not literally running around inside a wheel designed for exercising pet hamsters, this type of expression is not considered a fundamental component of language. Such figures of speech are at best poetically pertinent and useful for specific purposes, but are nonetheless linguistically peripheral.

Another traditional distinction is between living and dead or frozen metaphors. A living metaphor is in some sense new or at least obvious as being a figure of speech, as opposed to something meant literally. When poet Tomas Tranströmer writes "constellations stamping inside their stalls" (Tranströmer, 2011, p. 4), it is obvious to his readers that he is speaking figuratively, "as if" the constellations are stallions, impatiently pawing the ground. Compare this to someone saying that she feels "down" or "empty." These expressions are so well established or so conventional that the listener often understands them as literal and the original metaphorical character can seem nonexistent. Simply saying that a metaphor is dead or frozen is, of course, yet another instance of the same phenomenon. The example of the hamster wheel can be living or dead: in some circumstances we might assume that the metaphorical nature of the phrase is obvious, but it is also possible that both the speaker and the listener only connect with its literal signification of "having too much to do." The terms "open" and "closed" are also sometimes used to distinguish between new and conventional metaphors.

Further subdivisions are sometimes made of the category of words and phrases that I have generally referred to as metaphors. The above example of the White House is what is termed a *metonym*, which is when one thing (the US president) is identified by reference to a closely associated phenomenon (his residence). Saying that you enjoy Bertolt Brecht when meaning, in a literal sense, that you like reading plays written by Brecht is also a case of a metonym. Another, closely related term is *synecdoche*. This is a figure of speech by which we talk about something by reference to a part of that thing. An example might be saying "we had many mouths to feed" instead of that there were many people there. Another frequently used term is *simile*, which is a figure of speech involving a comparison between two things. Saying "his house is a dump" is, in this definition, a metaphor, but if we add a word signifying the comparative aspect ("his house is *like* a dump"), it is sometimes called a simile.

These types of distinction are especially common in more philosophical and conventionally linguistic texts and play no major role in the empirical metaphor research that interests me in this book. Besides, the inter-category boundaries are vague and often meaningless to my purposes, so they will not be used.

Another term that is used a little variably in scientific texts is *analogy*, which is often taken to be synonymous enough with metaphor as for the two to be interchangeable. Sometimes, however, analogy is regarded as a broader linguistic phenomenon, of which metaphor is a subcategory. This is a terminological application that becomes meaningful from the perspective of relational frame theory, since this form of theory allows us to specify what distinguishes a metaphor from other kinds of analogy. I will be returning to this in chapter 4.

Source and Target

Already Aristotle, then, was describing metaphor as the transposition of an original signifier onto another, as expressed even in the etymology of the Greek *metaphorá*, where *meta* means "over" and *phero* "to carry": thus "to carry over." We may use the expression "He's just a big teddy bear" as a simple illustration. One thing is assumed known (what a big teddy bear is like) and the person thus described becomes known in some sense through the "carrying over" of what already applied to large teddy bears to him. Similarly, the metaphor "She's a real terrier" assumes knowledge of the character of a terrier, and therefore something is now known, through the agency of the metaphor, about the person. A phenomenon is assumed to be more known in one or other respect, and its properties transferred in some sense to another phenomenon, where the former is usually referred to as the metaphor's vehicle, base, or source (the teddy bear/the terrier) and the latter its target (the man/the woman). In "my boss is a nagging old fishwife," "my boss" is the target, a "nagging old fishwife" the source; in "it feels like a heavy weight on my shoulders," the speaker's feelings are the metaphor's target and heavy weight resting on somebody's shoulders its source. The concepts of source and target to denote the two parts of the metaphor are common in metaphor scholarship regardless of specific theory, and I will be following this praxis.

Conceptual Metaphors

In 1980, linguist George Lakoff and philosopher Mark Johnson published *Metaphors We Live By*, a book that has proved seminal to modern ideas of metaphors and heavily influenced research in the fields of linguistics, psychology, and cognitive science. The primary aim of the book is to challenge the idea that metaphors are secondary phenomena in language and cognition. Instead, the authors argue that metaphors are absolutely fundamental to the human condition and that we actually live our lives through them. Metaphors are more basic than literal language. To quote David Leary: "All knowledge is ultimately rooted in metaphorical (or analogical) modes of perception and thought" (Leary, 1990, p. 2). This argument derives from a universal, natural experience: when we encounter something new, we always interpret it in relation to something already known. If the new thing is a word, we seek other words through which to understand it; if the thing is an event or an experience, we place it in relation to similar occasions through which we may make sense of it. Understanding the new through the agency of the known is absolutely fundamental. This view also relativizes the difference between a literal and a metaphorical language. Even if it can be practical to distinguish these two in many instances, the difference is by no means unambiguous. We could put it like this: the ability to symbolize (to have one thing stand for another) is the very bedrock of language.

According to Lakoff and Johnson (1980), we live our lives on the basis of what they call *conceptual metaphors*, which are fundamental metaphors that exert a powerful influence over our way of thinking, speaking, and acting. These metaphors are ultimately rooted in the experience of our own bodies and of negotiating our surroundings. A simple example of this is "up is good, down is bad," a conceptual metaphor that is presumed to lie at the heart of such expressions as "things have been going downhill recently," "he has a high work capacity," and "the mood at the meeting was pretty low," and explains the significance of gestures such as "thumbs up" or "thumbs down."

Another example of a conceptual metaphor is life as journey, which informs such expressions as "you've come to a crossroads," "our paths crossed," "education provides an important start in life," and "I'm delighted to have come this far" (often said in reference to a professional life). Other examples are:

- Argument is war. ("Your position is totally indefensible"; "His argument was easy to shoot down"; "She kept attacking my views.")

- Life is a game. ("The odds are against me"; "If I play my cards right…"; "She drew the short straw.")

- Ideas are objects. ("Bring that to our next meeting"; "Will you please drop that?")

- Ideas are food. ("I find that hard to swallow"; "It was something to get my teeth into.")

- Ideas are goods. ("You'll have to try to sell him that"; "Your idea is completely worthless.")

- Theories are buildings. ("It was a theory built on sand"; "That's where your theory falls to the ground"; "That's the basis of the entire theory.")

- The mind is a machine. ("He's got a screw loose"; "I feel totally rusty"; "That got the old cogs working.")

- Influence is a physical force. ("I couldn't resist the pressure"; "What she said really made an impact on me"; "And on that bombshell...")

These researchers and theoreticians thus maintain that metaphors are not primarily figures of speech denoting a literal meaning, but a kind of "collective subconscious" that influences how we experience our lives, how we think, and how we express ourselves, and as such are conceptual rather than linguistic. Much of the research is devoted to identifying figures of speech, comparing languages and language regions, and empirical study in one form or another (see Gibbs, 2008, for a comprehensive account). It is assumed that metaphors are based on the human need to relate to and talk about abstract and nebulous phenomena, onto which we therefore project more concrete and specific experiences.

One instance of a universal concept that has been the object of much experimental study is how we talk about time in spatial terms (Boroditsky, 2000). We speak as if we move relative to time ("We're heading toward better days") or time moves relative to us ("Summer will soon be here"). Our concrete experience is that things continually change in a particular direction and the idea that "time" has a direction seems common to all cultures. Talking about time with the help of spatial metaphors thus appears to be a ubiquitous cultural phenomenon, although the actual spatial metaphors used differ. How does time move? Forward? Backward? Does it move up or down? Studies of different cultures and language groups reveal much variation here. In English (and Swedish) we usually refer to time as if it moved horizontally relative to us ("Our best years are ahead of us"). In Mandarin, the largest Chinese language, people speak as if time moved vertically (next month is "down" and the previous month is "up") (Boroditsky, 2001). What the languages have in common, however, is the use of a spatial metaphor. We also talk about ideas as things and about organizations as if they were plants ("Our company is growing fast"). From this we can infer that the source phenomena are often more tangible and the target phenomena abstract or relatively indistinct. I will now explore such an area, one which we may also assume to be of particular psychotherapeutic significance.

Conceptual Metaphors and Emotions

Included among the fields that often serve as targets for metaphors, according to linguistic analysts, are our different emotional states and experiences. Notice, incidentally, the term "emotional state," as if our emotions were able to adopt different positions or locations in space. This is assumed to be connected with (Again! I shall have to stop pointing out all the metaphors that creep in [!] to the text lest I do so *ad nauseum*) the fact that we find emotions harder to grasp or define than many external things that are more tangible or distinct (Kövecses, 2002). This analysis is also close to that made by Skinner as regards how we learn to speak about what he calls "private events." I will be returning to this in chapter 3. However, modern linguistic research concurs that the way in which we talk about feelings works in just this way. Phenomena that are more tangible and better defined than emotions are used as sources for metaphors that have emotions as their targets. Most of the studies conducted in this respect have concerned the English language, which has hundreds of metaphor-based expressions relating to emotions. The same applies to my language, Swedish, too. In Sweden, we are "ice cold with fear"; we "boil over with anger"; we are "shot into space" with elation; we are "filled up" with joy or "heavy" with grief; we can feel "shaken up," "touched," or "down-tuned (dejected)"; we can "tingle" with curiosity; we "swell" with pride; and we can feel "empty." We burst into laughter, we vent our anger, we hunger for love, we burn with interest, and we float with joy.

In modern linguistic analyses of these everyday, metaphorical ways of expressing feelings, it is often maintained that such language is based on conceptual metaphors that not only are figures of speech but provide models upon which we also think and act. One such fundamental conceptual emotional metaphor is that emotions are forces (Kövecses, 2010). This is also intimated by the very etymology of the word *emotion,* which derives from the Latin for "out of, from" (*e*) and "to move" (*movere*); in other words, out of something that moves. (The Swedish word *sinnesrörelse*—literally "mental movement"—is even more explicit in this regard!)

One issue that is often discussed in linguistic texts is the extent to which these conceptual metaphors are either universal or specific to a certain language or language family (Schnall, 2014). The theory that conceptual metaphors are based on the experience of our own bodies and the fact that we interact with our surroundings seems to suggest that they are—up to a point, at least—universal. There is much research to illustrate this.

The conceptual metaphor "anger is contained pressure" is a variation on the "emotions are forces" theme, and has been the subject of much study in a number of languages. In both English and Swedish, we boil and explode with anger, we seethe, we try to contain our anger, and we can have an outburst of rage. In cartoon strips, anger is often depicted as a little cloud of something (steam? smoke?) coming out of the figure's ears, as if erupting from his head as a sudden release of pent-up pressure. This very type of conceptual metaphor— anger is contained pressure—is demonstrable in many other languages unrelated to Anglo-Nordic. Hungarian, Chinese, Japanese, Tahitian, and Wolof (spoken in West Africa), metaphorize anger in these terms (Kövecses, 2002.). It is not claimed that all conceptual metaphors are universal, but that many are very widespread, including some describing emotional states. While it could be argued that this relative ubiquity is due merely to linguistic contagion, it is our experience of our own bodies and their physiological makeup that is held as the most probable cause.

Emotions are thus an area that we often talk about with the help of metaphors. And we may presume that the fact that emotions are often central to psychotherapeutic practice is why metaphors are used more often in psychotherapeutic conversation than in many other situations in which we communicate with each other. Emotions bring the subject of metaphors up for discussion, so to speak.

Conceptual Metaphors and Gestures

I mentioned previously that conceptual metaphors are assumed to influence not only spoken language and thinking but also other kinds of human action, such as gesturing. Folding the fingers into the palm while extending the thumb upward ("thumbs up") is an almost universal gesture for "good" (Müller & Cienki, 2009). While it is not common to all languages, its notional opposite ("down is good") does not exist anywhere (Lakoff, 1993). Again, it is assumed that the background to this conceptual metaphor and its different concrete expression is our shared experience of our physical world since time immemorial: pouring liquid into a receptacle or gathering objects into a pile creates a very real sensation of "more is up." What we want more of is good; hence, "up is good."

In recent years, linguists have taken such an approach to studying human communication through physical images (in advertising, film, propaganda, and so forth) and gestures, and how these modes of communication co-vary with speech (Cienki & Müller, 2008; Forceville, 2009). These studies also seem to support the notion that shared metaphors (either for a specific community or more generally) are implicit and inform both image use and gestures effectively in the same way as they do language. It is often said that gestures and "body language" are a fundamentally different means of communication from the spoken and written word, even to the extent that they derive from different areas of the brain. Both linguistic research and more recent brain research suggest otherwise (Cardillo et al., 2012; Giora, 2008; Yus, 2009). The same conceptual metaphors can be traced in both speech and gestures, and the use of metaphor in general seems also to overlap rather than distinguish itself from more literal language. The theory of different brain centers for metaphors on the one hand and literal language on the other is outdated (Coulson, 2008)— further indication that the classic distinction between literal and metaphorical language has a very limited bearing on reality.

Modern linguistic research describes different theoretical ways in which gestures and speech can interact, specifically with regard to metaphor use (Müller, 2008; Cienki & Müller, 2008):

- A spoken phrase and a simultaneous gesture can reflect the same metaphor (in other words, the source and the target are the same for both). An example of this is when someone says "You have to weigh your options" while cupping both hands and waving them gently up and down in mimicry of a pair of old-fashioned scales.

- A spoken metaphor and a simultaneous gestured metaphor also commonly have the same target but different sources. An example of this is a discussion in which one person criticizes the opinions of another by saying, "You make it sound as if it's all just black and white—surely there's some grey too?" while holding both hands out, separating them toward their respective sides (left hand to the left, right hand to the right) and pointing them briefly away from each other; and then, when mentioning "some grey," bringing the hands closer and waggling them at each other. Both of these metaphors have the other person's opinions as target, but the spoken one has recourse to contrasting shades (black, white, and grey) as a source, while the gestured one is spatial.

- Spoken and gestured metaphors can also, of course, be used independently of one another. Just as we can say something metaphorical without gesturing metaphorically, so can we gesture metaphorically while speaking literally. An example of this is when someone says "You know exactly what I mean" while pointing an index finger at an imaginary object in front of her ("ideas as things").

Research into gestures and their place in human communication is an extensive field in its own right and is also likely to have relevance for psychotherapeutic communication. Any further exploration of this is, however, beyond the intended scope of this book. My point in touching upon the importance and metaphorical source of gestures is to illustrate how fundamental metaphors are to human communication and how they cannot be confined to a particular aspect of language. Indeed, they constitute its very bedrock.

Cognitive Linguistics

The linguists who have, since the 1980s (and since Lakoff and Johnson's groundbreaking book), adopted the theory of conceptual metaphors as the bases of speech, gesture, and image use call themselves cognitive linguists (Kövecses, 2010; Lakoff, 1993). They emphasize that the cognitive (thinking) is more fundamental than the spoken, the traditional focus of linguists. It is the reason for the emphasis on conceptual metaphors, which assume the existence of implicit structures underlying the directly observable: namely that we use metaphorical language or gesticulate in a particular way. It is common for these authors to polemicize directly with what has historically dominated linguistics, namely a careful analysis of the specifically spoken. They write things like "metaphor is fundamentally conceptual, not linguistic, in nature," "the locus of metaphor is not in language at all, but in the way we conceptualize one mental domain in terms of another" (Lakoff, 1993, pp. 203, 244), and "we thus need to distinguish conceptual metaphor from metaphorical linguistic expressions" (Kövecses, 2010, p. 4). They describe concrete metaphorical statements as superficial manifestations of underlying conceptual metaphors. The metaphors actually uttered intimate the existence of these underlying structures, and it is these latter on which their analysis pivots.

Within the bounds of this view, conceptual metaphors are described in a way that largely coincides with how cognitive theorists generally use the term *schemata* or *mental representations*. They observe what people say or do and postulate underlying structures that are assumed to control what one can directly observe. Like cognitive theory as a whole, cognitive linguists have recently approached neurobiology in the hope of describing, with its help, these assumed underlying structures (Lakoff, 2008).

Readers familiar with a behavioral analytic outlook know that it clashes with the above assumptions. I and many others have already described how behavioral analysts have repudiated the postulated idea of inner structures as an explanatory model for human action (Ramnerö & Törneke, 2008; Skinner, 1974; Törneke, 2010; Wilson, 2001), so rather than going through it all again I will merely cite a pragmatic reason for seeking a different description: if we, in our pursuit of psychotherapy, are to use metaphors to understand and influence, it is what is actually done and said, what we can observe, that we must focus on—simply because it is all we have direct access to.

At the same time as behavior analysis has good reason to be critical of the theoretical assumptions of cognitive linguistics, it does not mean that we must necessarily overlook the phenomena that these scholars describe. Explanatory models are one thing, the phenomena they try to explain another (Fryling, 2013). And the phenomena cognitive linguists describe seem robust. People use metaphors in the way cognitive linguists describe, and this use appears cardinal to the way we experience our lives. The way we communicate with each other, be it orally or otherwise, is very much dominated by metaphors. Areas of particular relevance to psychotherapy, such as talking about feelings and other "inner" phenomena, also seem to be especially marked by metaphor. Behavior analysis has a historical tendency to ignore research with different points of departure from its own. I think that this is a mistake and easily leads us astray. On the contrary, it is important for us to observe phenomena from perspectives other than our own and see how much a behavior analytical approach can contribute to scientific advancement.

The Effects of Metaphor

Let me end this first chapter with a brief account of a series of experiments illustrating the powerful impact a metaphor can make on us. In 2011 and 2013, Thibodeau and Boroditsky presented a group of a few hundred people with a short story about a fictional city (Addison) by way of experiment. The city was described as prosperous up until a few years ago, when the crime rate increased. The text as presented to half of the group began "Crime is a virus ravaging the city…" and then continued to describe the situation with statistics on the rising crime rate; the text presented to the other group began "Crime is a beast ravaging the city…" before delving into the same statistics as the first. After having read the text, the participants were asked to answer two questions about possible policy responses for reducing crime in Addison: "In your view, what action does Addison need to take to reduce the crime rate?" and "What roles should the police have in Addison?" The differences between the responses of the two groups were clear. When the questions were open-ended, 81 percent of the "beast" group suggested a higher police presence, for example, in contrast to only 31 percent of the "virus" group. When participants in an identical experiment were asked about areas to investigate and had to choose between improving economic welfare/reforming education on the one hand, and harsher prison sentences/more police patrols on the other, the difference between the groups was equally striking. Generally speaking, metaphorically framing crime as a "beast" led to proposals to arresting and imprisoning criminals, whereas metaphorically framing crime as a "virus" encouraged people to seek causes and propose socially-oriented solutions (reduce poverty and improve education).

The researchers also asked the participants to tell them what had influenced their proposals. Only a small percentage of them mentioned the metaphorical expression. In both groups, the vast majority referred to the statistics presented in the text (both versions of which, apart from the fourth word, were identical). In some subsidiary studies, participants were asked explicitly about the metaphor by having them fill in the missing word in the text they had read: "Crime is a … ravaging the city." Approximately half the participants were able to recall the metaphor they had read ("virus" or "beast"), but their ability or failure to do so did not correlate with the answers they had given to proposed crime-reducing measures. The researchers concluded that the influence of the metaphor was independent of whether or not the participants were consciously aware of it.

Another follow-up experiment is worth a mention. Here, the researchers moved the opening sentence, which contained the only word that distinguished the texts, to the end. As a result, the difference in responses between the two groups noted in the other follow-up experiment disappeared.[2] The researchers concluded from this that the demonstrated effect does not depend on a simple association made by the participants when answering the questions (if this were the case, the immediacy effect would have been more evident) but that the metaphor, when given initially, influences their reading and understanding of the entire narrative. To echo Lakoff and Johnson: these were metaphors on the basis of which the participants read, understood, and expressed themselves.

Other experiments have shown similar results on metaphor use and its influence on other action. In one illustrative study, the researchers asked the participants to read comments on current share trends, describing them as rising using either an active "agent" metaphor ("the share price climbed higher") or a passive "object" one ("the share price was pushed higher"). They then showed that when the participants had to predict the future share price, the people in the "agent" group were more likely to say that it would continue to rise than those in the "object" group (Morris, Sheldon, Ames, & Young, 2007).

Conclusion

Metaphors are more fundamental to language and cognition than has traditionally been assumed. They are not just "linguistic ornamentation" used by

---

2 Each experiment used different participants.

poets and rhetoricians, but the building blocks of language and cognition in general. We integrate constantly with each other and with our surroundings in a way that is markedly affected by our use of metaphors. We "live on the basis" of these metaphors and they govern our actions. Modern linguistics contains a great deal of knowledge about the structure and mechanism of this phenomenon, and we have much to learn of its analyses, even if we have other theoretical premises than those that have dominated linguistic research since the 1980s. I will be returning to how behavior analysis can tackle the phenomenological field described in this chapter, but before that we shall spend a little time on parts of linguistic research that depart from the view outlined above. For it turns out that there are linguists today who adopt positions that in many ways tally with the claims of behavior analysis.

CHAPTER 2

Metaphors—in Context

Cognitive linguistics in general and the theory of conceptual metaphors in particular direct focus onto assumed "metaphor schema" that often seem independent of the context in which a concrete metaphorical expression is used. Cognitive research looks at metaphors that are actually spoken, but does so primarily in order to see indications of assumed, underlying conceptual metaphors. In practice, they are therefore in danger of overlooking important factors regarding actually used metaphorical expressions, such as what influences their use and what effects this has on human interaction. There is no inevitable conflict between describing the common metaphorical patterns or themes and studying how people use metaphors in practice. However, in recent years many linguists have claimed that the theory of conceptual metaphors is limited and incomplete, precisely because it provides no tools for examining actually used metaphors and the situations in which they are used. We will now be looking a little more closely at some of these contributions.

Metaphors in Human Interaction

Metaphors are used in connection not only with other phrases or gestures but also with social, cultural, and communicative contexts. Metaphor use, like other forms of communication, is never context free. The most basic context is one of interaction between individuals. Look at the following pair of situations, which make formal use of the same metaphor:

Two colleagues are discussing their workplace. The first one says, "I hate how we never get to have a say around here. Paul always decides things while the rest of us just have to do as we're told." The other replies, "Right, Paul is the captain of this ship all right."

Compare this with the first person saying, "It's been pretty chaotic here recently—lucky that Paul has a grip on things," and the second replying, "Right, Paul is the captain of this ship all right."

The same metaphor (Paul as captain) is used in the two examples, but denotes different things. Not only does a metaphor acquire meaning from how it is constructed, but the context in which it is used also influences its function for the listener and thus the sense with which it received. In these two examples, the metaphor source (the captain of a ship) has two different functions. In the first, the captain's role as decision maker and unchallengeable leader is brought into negative focus ("he steamrolls us; we have no influence, no freedom"), while the second puts a positive spin on his role as resourceful leader, savior even ("he makes sure that things work; he'll get us through all this"), despite it being the same metaphor. It is thus not just the source and target of a metaphor that gives it meaning; the context in which it is used also makes a critical contribution to its signification (Ritchie, 2006; Wee, 2005).

In many ways, the theory of conceptual metaphors challenged linguistic research. The scientific field of linguistics comprises people's actual way of speaking, and its metaphor research has thus focused on how metaphors are used as a feature of human speech. Cognitive linguistics shifted the focus onto presumed cognitive structures that operated automatically, often without the speaker being aware of it. When we say "prices have risen recently" or "he's behind in his studies," it is not as if we are making a deliberate choice to express what we mean in metaphorical terms of "up is more" or "life as journey." We speak as if these metaphors are taken for granted. The linguists who have recently questioned cognitive linguistics in general and conceptual metaphors in particular do not deny this or the importance of Lakoff and Johnson's work. But to their way of thinking, the emphasis on underlying (or overarching) abstracted metaphors risks missing what can be learned from studying actual metaphorical expressions and the contexts in which they are used. In many ways, this emphasis naturally relates to the focus that behavior analysis places on concrete behavior and the context in which this behavior occurs. The crux of the matter is the significance of the context, and "metaphorizing" as actual speech. I will present some important implications of this observation under five headings: the need for multidisciplinary analysis; language influences thought; metaphors as product and process; dead metaphors revived; and intentional metaphor use.

The Need for an Interdisciplinary Analysis

Cognitive linguistics as formulated by Lakoff and Johnson as well as Kövecses (2002; 2010) places considerable emphasis on assumed cognitive schema in the form of metaphors, which are referred to as conceptual. The wording of these metaphors thus becomes critical, since they are assumed to govern how we think and act. They easily become "carved in stone." Consider, for example, the conceptual metaphor of "argument is war." We often express ourselves as if such as metaphor were a given: "She shot his argument out of the sky"; "He crushed all opposition in the debate"; "We opened the discussion with a frontal assault"; and so forth. But does this mean that we are necessarily using the concept of war as a source? When such a conventionalized expression is used, is it self-evident that a conceptual metaphor is influencing the interaction? Imagine that a child grows up without any immediate contact with war but in an environment where arguments are common and where war is a mere game experienced via a games console. Is it not reasonable to presume that expressions like "he crushed all his opponents" will be interpreted differently from a metaphor with actual war as its source (Steen, 2011)? Is it not more reasonable to posit a historical development, where even central, abstracted metaphorical themes change over time under the influence of multiple historical and contextual factors (Gentner & Bowdle, 2008)?

Historical, social, and cultural knowledge seems important for preventing our understanding and use of metaphors from becoming oversimplified; in other words, the theory of conceptual metaphors is in danger of becoming reductionist. We risk reading too much into a figure of speech that might be expressing something entirely different from what we think we hear. If metaphorical forms of expression are also a vital and essential part of communication, we might stray in our scientific analysis. Another aspect of this same argument is that the admittedly important observation that a metaphor's source can often be traced to the human body and our concrete interaction with our environment can be reductionist. There is a danger that this observation distracts us from cultural and individual factors when we try to figure out what serves as the source of a given metaphor.

A similar danger is posed by neurobiological reductionism. As with cognitive theory in general, the step for cognitive linguists to neurobiological explanatory models is a short one (Lakoff, 2008). That neurobiology has an important contribution to make to our understanding of human behavior, which reasonably includes the use of metaphors, goes without saying. At the same time, however, its oft-dominant position can lure one into reductionism (in other words, everything human is reduced to brain function) and away from important scientific knowledge about how we interact with each other and our environment, and the influence this has on how we use metaphors (Ritchie, 2006; Steen, 2011).

The theory of conceptual metaphors—by which I mean underlying or overarching metaphorical themes that fundamentally shape human action—need not be reductionist. But it does need to offset with a study of how people actually use metaphors in a concrete historical context.

Language Influences Thought

In cognitive linguistics, the thought is primary to the spoken. At the same time, we now have reams of empirical research showing that our concrete language, like the language we use, very much affects how we think and generally act. Part of this research has its focus on metaphors. As I mentioned in chapter 1, it is common for people to relate to the concept of time through spatial metaphors. The past is behind us, the future is ahead of us; for time—at least as is most usually the case in English (and Swedish)—sits upon a horizontal axis (backward/forward, left/right). Yet there are language groups that see time as something based on fixed external coordinates, such as points of the compass, or permanent features of the environment, such as rivers delineating the language group's traditional habitat (Fedden & Boroditsky, 2012). Mandarin uses both spatial metaphors that have time pass along a horizontal axis, as English does, but also a vertical axis, so that the future is down and the past up. Repeated studies have shown that people who speak only English relate to time as if it moved horizontally in nonlinguistic tests as well, and that people whose mother tongue is Mandarin very much relate to time as if it also moved vertically. This can be tested by, for example, showing people images depicting a course of events (a piece of fruit at different stages of being eaten, or a famous person at different ages) and asking them to indicate "before and after" by pointing to or moving a cursor on a computer screen. Alternatively, a researcher might stand beside the participant so that both are facing the same direction, hold out a hand palm-upwards (as if holding something) and say, "If this is lunch, where would you put breakfast?" Or, if the experiment is taking place in

September, "If this is September, where would you put October?" The participant is then instructed to indicate his answer with a silent gesture, and the researcher makes note of the direction in which the participant understands time to "move."

The results of such experiments show that people interact with their experience of time in accordance with their linguistic convention, even when not speaking (Fuhrman, McGormick, Chen, Jiang, Shu, Mao, & Boroditsky, 2011). In another series of experiments, Fuhrman and coworkers looked at different groups of people who spoke both Mandarin and English, but at various levels of proficiency. What they found was that the more fluent someone is in Mandarin, the more likely she is to place time on a vertical axis. When people fluent in both languages were tested, they also found that the language used by the researchers in the actual test situation (when giving instructions, say) affected the results; if they spoke English, the participants were more likely to act as if time moved horizontally, and if they spoke Mandarin, they were more likely to interact with time as a vertical phenomenon. This can also be influenced by other contextual factors, such as images with a distinct linguistic localization.

There are also experiments that look into other parameters of the spoken language, such as grammatical praxis, to see how much they influence thought (Boroditsky, Schmidt, & Phillips, 2003; Fausey & Boroditsky, 2011). One example of this is the different praxis surrounding gender. In Spanish and German, substantives have gender; some are feminine, others are masculine. The researchers selected words that are feminine in German and masculine in Spanish, and vice versa, and then studied how the participants (who speak one language or the other) interact with certain objects. Doing this, they have shown that when one of the language groups is asked to specify the properties of an object, adjectives that are culturally more masculine will be ascribed to the masculine gendered objects, and more feminine qualities will be attributed to objects that are of the feminine gender. Put simply: people who speak Spanish see keys as being feminine and bridges as masculine and relate to them as such in a wide variety of ways; German speakers, on the other hand, see bridges and keys the other way round. All of this is derived from the grammatical gender each word has in the respective language. One interesting result is that it can be shown that gender congruity affects powers of observation. Researchers showed people pairs of photographs, one of a person of distinct gender and one of an object of either the same or the opposite grammatical gender, and then asked them to describe similarities between the person and the object. The photographs were then arranged so that there were similarities between the two, irrespective of gender. Doing this, the researchers demonstrated that people notice the similarities much more if the genders match than if they do not.

Other grammatical differences between languages are also thought to influence us. For instance, it has been shown that different grammatical praxis between English and Spanish regarding how people commonly describe accidents (in English, the person involved is often spoken about in active terms, while in Spanish, the person is usually passive) influences recall. We remember different things in a given chain of events depending, in part, on the language we speak (Fausey & Boroditsky, 2011).

Our concrete speech, the language we speak, is thus not just a tool with which to express our thoughts; on the contrary, what we think and how we generally act is shaped by our concrete linguistic praxis.

Metaphors as Process and Product

A study of general, common conceptual metaphors easily leads us to focus on metaphors as products, on their content. If someone says "the sales trend is heading upwards" or "he upped his game," either metaphor reflects the conceptual metaphor of "up is good." But even if we do not assume that the analysis is always important for each occasion when some such thing is said, the observation leaves many questions unanswered. What happens when utterances like this are spoken? Using a metaphor is an action, something we do: we "metaphorize." What does this process look like? How do we create metaphors? And in what circumstances and with what consequences do we speak metaphorically?

Frankfurt professor Cornelia Müller is a leading linguist and metaphor researcher. She stresses that metaphors are not to be studied merely as a cognitive product but as something we do, a cognitive activity (Müller, 2008). And to understand this human activity we have to study when it is performed, when we "metaphorize." With this emphasis on the creation and use of metaphors, Müller hooks up more generally with modern trends in cognitive science, which holds cognition to be an activity, a form of sensorimotor skill, rather than a representational process (Chemero, 2009; Noë, 2004) This view also coheres with behavior analysis, and to its understanding of concrete action in a certain historical context. "Cognitive processes are behavioral processes; they are things people do" (Skinner, 1989, p. 17).

Dead Metaphors Revived

The traditional discussion about metaphors has toned down the type of metaphor that has been called "dead," "frozen," or "petrified" in favor of the metaphors considered "living." A typical example of the latter is new metaphors, such as those used in poetry, where one entity is linked to another in a new, unexpected way: "Awakening is a parachute jump from the dream" (Tranströmer, 2011, p. 3). Dead metaphors are expressions that have become so common or conventionalized that they have lost their metaphorical function and joined the ranks of the literal. An obvious example of this is the word I have just used when I wrote that expressions have "lost" their metaphorical function. The sense of "losing meaning" is hardly something we now consider metaphorical, even if, with a little reflection, we can see that it at least has a metaphorical root.

The theory of conceptual metaphors turned this traditional view on its head (!). It was argued that these "dead" metaphors were not at all that defunct, nor had they lost their metaphorical function. On the contrary, they very much influence human action through precisely their metaphorical nature. They are based on fundamental, conceptual metaphors that are the very bedrock of human cognition, and their influence is largely unconscious, or at the very least spontaneous. Since it is these conceptual metaphors that have the greatest impact on our lives, it is, contrary to the claims of the traditionalists, these "dead" metaphors that deserve to be the object of research.

Even though research has changed tack since the 1980s from the traditional view to that of the conceptual metaphor, there is, paradoxically, one thing that has been preserved: the given distinction between petrified or dead metaphors on the one hand, and the living or new on the other. Focus has shifted with regard to their respective meanings, but the traditional classification has been kept. One consequence of the recent research focus—the more intensive study of how metaphors are actually used in their contexts—is the insight that this distinction is in many respects illusory. It is more the case that dead metaphors are often "revived" in everyday dialogue. By studying actual conversations, one can look for markers for whether a dead, conventionalized metaphor actually has a metaphorical influence or not. Simply because someone uses language that can be seen to have a martial source ("I shot his argument down in flames") it does not necessarily mean that she is doing so from the conceptual metaphorical framing of "argument is war." The expression can, for the individual, be completely empty of its possible metaphorical content and merely mean "I had a more logical argument." To ascertain whether there is a metaphorical function one must analyze a given episode, or how a certain expression is used in a certain context. Müller describes a clear example of when such a metaphorical function seems to have existed despite the highly conventionalized nature of the actual verbal expression (2008, s. 77, ff.).

The example, from an actual conversation, concerns the first love of a woman now in her forties. She relates how she fell in love with a boy in her class on a school outing. While she describes the occasion in positive terms, she says that the trip was "overshadowed" by his "depressiveness." When saying the word "depressiveness," she moves her open right palm down is if pushing something downwards. She makes this gesture twice. Müller points out two things: the word *depressive* derives from the Latin for "press down." It is, however, a highly conventionalized metaphor and the woman was not familiar with the word's etymology. Secondly, she uses no other verbal utterance during the conversation embodying this sense of "sad is down," yet still uses a downward-pressing gesture. It seems as if, in this very real situation, a "dead" metaphorical expression has been brought back to life. In Müller's phraseology, "a sleeping metaphor awoke."

The main point that Müller and other scholars make in their criticism of the conceptual metaphor theory is that it is only through the study of actual events that metaphorical function can be examined, and that it is not enough for the content of a phrase to enable such an interpretation. The fact that a certain metaphor is produced does not necessarily imply a metaphorical process. Content is one thing, function another. To establish that an expression has a certain function, it must be analyzed in the context in which it is uttered.

Further questions present themselves. If the woman's gesture as she talks of her first love indicates that a sleeping metaphor has been woken, what, in the context, woke it up? Müller's analysis of the conversation provides no answer.

She does, however, discuss questions of a more principle kind, such as: What does a metaphorical process look like? What characterizes it and how does it interact with the context in which it operates? Since relational frame theory offers some answers to these questions, I will be returning to them in chapter 4.

In the previous example, the use of a metaphorical expression seems to have been unintentional. But if sleeping metaphors can be woken, it begs another interesting question: can they be made so intentionally in a dialogue, and if so, how can this be done?

Intentional Metaphor Use

A reasonable conclusion of modern metaphor research is that the classification of metaphors as either dead or alive is unviable. Metaphors as specific expressions (metaphors as product) exist rather along a continuum, from historically so conventionalized that they are unrecognized as such by most users, to completely novel metaphorical inventions. Near to one end of this continuum is the word referred to above: *depressiveness*. Another is the word *emotion*, the etymology of which—"out of something that moves"—is wholly irrelevant to most users. Müller calls this type of metaphor "opaque." The example from Tomas Tranströmer's poem on awakening being a parachute jump from the dream is at the other end of this continuum. It is completely "transparent" as a metaphor in that anyone encountering it would understand its metaphorical nature. However, most metaphorical expressions exist somewhere between these two extremes. Expressions that have become highly conventionalized through a long history of usage can still be transparent in this sense—to "praise someone to the skies," or to "run round and round in a hamster wheel," for instance. As illustrated by the woman and her first love, completely opaque metaphorical expression can also influence our actions.

The question of intentionality in the use of metaphors cannot be fully answered in terms of how opaque or transparent a metaphor is. Intentionality is no inherent quality of a metaphor, but a way of referring to the action of the person who utters it. Still, some clues are provided by the continuum, since at the transparent end one might reasonably assume that a new metaphor is used intentionally. In fact, it is hard to imagine an instance when this is not the case. The metaphor can, however, naturally be "sleeping" for the listener in the sense that it is not grasped or does not influence.

For speakers who wish to influence people through the intentional use of metaphor it is therefore natural to create new ones. Given that metaphorical language is so fundamental to communication and the inevitable transparency of a new metaphor (assuming it is understood as such by the listener), it is very likely that the speaker will trigger a metaphorical process in the listener, for the very reason that the metaphor is new. If the metaphor is new, it will be construed as metaphorical. This presumably explains why new metaphors are often used in rhetorics and literature, both of which are explicitly intended to influence. The same applies to psychological therapy, and could give therapists good reason to create new metaphors of relevance to the therapeutic situation. As pointed out earlier, it seems that different therapeutic models concur that this is often a smart recourse. At the same time, we know that new metaphors are a tiny fraction of all the metaphorical expressions used in everyday interaction, perhaps as small as 1 percent (Steen, 2011). If metaphorical expressions are a vital part of communication in general and if most of these expressions are more or less conventionalized, an important influencing strategy is arguably to "awaken sleeping metaphors." A speaker can do this by deliberately using already established metaphors and referring to and developing metaphorical expressions that have already been employed by his conversational partner. I personally remember an episode from a therapy session I was in many years ago when, comparing my then new working situation with my previous one, I said, "This isn't exactly paradise either..." Upon which the psychologist said, "You're interested in that, in paradise?" The way in which she "woke" my relatively conventionalized metaphor led to what I found a helpful dialogue.

With this example from my own experience, this review of modern linguistic research and theory regarding metaphors settles neatly into the context of this book—the question of how metaphors can be used in psychotherapy. I will be returning to this in the clinical section.

Conclusion

The theory of conceptual metaphors has had a major impact on the linguistic analysis of metaphors, and is generally considered groundbreaking. At the same time, recent years' research has nuanced its claims, above all by emphasizing the analysis of actual metaphor use. One important conclusion that can be drawn so far is that the very process of "establishing or activating metaphoricity" (Müller, 2008, p. 215) must be made a field of study in its own right and that knowledge of the context in which this occurs is essential to greater scientific understanding. Another conclusion is that the classical dichotomy between dead and living metaphors is more of a continuum, along which the vast majority of metaphorical expressions are to varying degrees "sleeping" metaphors that exert a profound influence on human action and thought when "woken" through dialogue.

All this is arguably of much significance to the type of communication that takes place in the psychotherapist's room. Before I tackle these issues in earnest, I will return first to the book's theoretical premises, beginning with a historical overview of the dialogue on the phenomenon of metaphors within behavior analysis.

CHAPTER 3

Behavior Analysis and Metaphors

The main questions for behavior analysis are which factors, in a given historical situation, influence what someone does, and how these factors can be changed in order to affect behavior. The relationship between a specific act and the context in which it occurs is the point of interest. A typical *functional analysis* always begins with the question: What behavior do we want to analyze? Once this has been answered, the follow-up question is: What are the relevant factors in the moment that affect this behavior? And: How can we rearrange these factors to bring about a change in the behavior that is the object of our analysis?

This is an approach that is fairly simple in one sense, but that still requires a good deal of clarification lest it be misunderstood. The human behavior, or action, that one thus tries to assay is, in principal, anything done. In everyday parlance, the word *behavior* can have rather superficial associations. It is something that exists only "on the surface" and that is of a completely different essence to that which exists more "deep down." Human behavior is something "outer," in contrast to the human "inner." This is a definition that behavior analysts reject, as it is seen as a consequence of what in many respects are misleading metaphors that have been established over the centuries in our efforts to discuss the human condition (Skinner, 1989.) Contributing factors to this unfortunate classification are the subject of this book—the power of metaphor—and the human experience of being able to observe things in ourselves (physical sensations, thoughts, images, feelings) that are not as accessible to others. In many respects, it can of course be useful to talk about these experiences as "inner," but for a scientific understanding, behavior analysts argue that it is deceptive. So much so, that this area of human experience is conceived as being of a different kind, as if understandable through the agency of other principles than that which is called "outer." Historically, this is exactly what has happened; for centuries, this has been the domain of the "soul." The soul is a rare topic of scientific discussion these days, but the concept of the "psyche" and "mental phenomena" serve the same purpose: they intimate that these phenomena are of a different kind than can be regarded by an external observer. Behavior analysis, on the other hand, claims that these phenomena are to be understood with the help of the same principles as other human action. If we want to understand what someone remembers, feel or thinks, the same questions must be asked as when analyzing "outer" behavior: What are the feelings, thoughts, or memories we want to look at? And what are the relevant factors in the contexts when this person remembers, feels, or thinks? And how can we influence these factors if we desire change?

To repudiate all talk of the "inner" in this way is not to imply that these phenomena are trivial. That is not the point. It is *the way of talking about them* that behavior analysis decries. Indeed, the phenomena per se are often critical to understanding human behavior. And it is clear that we often tell people important things when using these words. When we say that "Steve puts his heart and soul" into a task, we are, of course, talking about something he is doing that we also take to be important to him. To say that "Ann's all heart" is no empty phrase, but says something about how she normally acts; no modern person would attribute her character to some quality of her physical heart. Saying that "Fatuma is mentally strong" is no meaningless claim either, as this also says something about how she normally behaves—perhaps her perseverance or ability to act in a crisis. However, it is misleading if it gives the impression that the person has a certain kind of "mental substance" that is a decisive factor in the behavior to which we are referring. Behavior analysts argue that these phenomena are best regarded as actions performed by the person under discussion, and if we wish to understand and influence, we need to analyze this behavior and its interaction with factors in the environment in which it is occurs. *The word "behavior" is thus used in behavior analysis about everything a person does.* Playing football, hating, remembering, withdrawing, grieving, playing the flute, giving up, feeling exhausted, jumping for joy—all these behaviors can be best understood if analyzed as acts performed in interaction with factors in the environment in which they occur. This is the premise of behavior analysis.

Yet another thing might need clarification, namely how we handle that which we usually refer to as "history." So far, my description of behavior analysis has focused on what happens in the here and now. What someone does is done in a given situation and the factors one is primarily interested in are the present factors at work. But what about the past? Is it not there that we must seek out the factors that influence the present? Yes, in one sense this goes without saying. We are the product of our experiences. If we want to find out why a certain skilled soccer player (such as Zlatan Ibrahimovic, a prominent Swedish player) plays soccer in the way he does, we must—besides perhaps assuming that he was born with what we like to call talent—look at how he learned to do so. And if we want to understand why a person suffers from anguish or avoids human contact, her past simply cannot be ignored. However, if we want not only to understand but also to influence Ibrahimovic's game, the current influencing factors acquire a particular salience. What does he do when dribbling? And what factors in the moment interact with his dribbling? That is where our final interest lies, for purely pragmatic reasons; it is governed by the simple fact that these factors are all that we have any real opportunity to change. The same reasoning applies to the kind of behavior that is the focus of psychotherapy. The current influencing factors are of particular practical interest.

The above argument on behavior, on the outer and inner, and on history and current influencing factors, derives from the theoretical position normally referred to as *functional contextualism* (Gifford & Hayes, 1999). The word *contextual* is used because it emphasizes the context of a given action, and the word *functional* is used because the main focus of interest is the function or the effect that contextual factors have on behavior.

The Importance of Consequences— in Language Too

"Men act upon the world, and change it, and are changed in turn by the consequences of their action" (Skinner, 1957, p. 1).

Thus begins Skinner's book on what he calls "verbal behavior," or what you and I would refer to as language. But it could also serve as the opening line to everything Skinner ever wrote, and to behavior analysis as a scientific discipline. One might also, however, describe the same process, but starting with the context in which "men" act, rather than the "men" themselves: "The world acts upon men, and changes their action, and the world is changed in turn by this action." Skinner begins with the acting human being for the simple reason that it is the scientific area that behavior analysis has made its own: predicting and influencing human behavior. But being able to start "from the other end" says something important: it is in the interaction between the acting person and the context in which she acts that both understanding and influence must be sought.

Skinner created what is often called *operant psychology*, the logical extension of the quote above. We operate on our environment and are changed by the consequences these operations have. A certain action has certain consequences, which influence the probability of a similar action happening again under similar circumstances. In a certain situation when Ibrahimovic gets the ball, he spins round, drags the ball back and to the right… In this, he interacts with a number of contextual factors, the interaction being influenced by previous consequences of similar actions. A man sees a person in uniform approach him on the pavement. His pulse starts to race, he starts to sweat, and perhaps he recalls previous occasions when he has had a similar physiological response; he stops, looks down, and turns toward a shop window and away from the uniformed figure. In this, he interacts with a number of contextual factors, the interaction being influenced by previous consequences of similar actions.

It is no coincidence that Skinner opens his book on language and how we interact verbally by writing something that could easily have introduced any of his other books. Human speech is also affected by consequences. When we say something, this too is an act that has consequences, consequences that influence how we continue to talk and generally how we act. This is the same as saying that language is operant behavior, and obeys, in many respects, the same principles of human action as other actions. So to return to the main theme of this book—metaphors—and to understand how behavior analysis has approached this subject, we must take a more general excursion into human language, especially language as operant behavior. Skinner broke responses down into different "verbal operants" on the basis of the particular way in which these responses interacted with the context in which they were spoken. I will here confine myself to describing the type of verbal operant he terms a *tact* (as in con*tact* or *tactile*) since it is within the frame of this phenomenon that he analyzes metaphor use. (For a fuller account of the different verbal operants Skinner describes, see Törneke, 2010, chapter 2.) This verbal operant he also describes as, in many respects, the most important.

Tacting—a Vital Skill

A tact is a verbal response that, apart from the previous consequences of similar responses, is influenced by something immediately preceding it. Someone uttering the response con*tacts* an object or an event. In Skinner's words: "A tact may be defined as a verbal operant in which a response of given form is evoked (or at least strengthened) by a particular object or event or property of an object or event" (Skinner 1957, pp. 81–82). The tacted activity is whatever immediately precedes the response. We often say "chair" when a chair is present. The response (what we say) is evoked by the chair. When we say "he's running," what we say is influenced by the presence of someone ("he") moving in a particular manner. Such responses are examples of what behavior analysis calls tacting. We tact our environment on the basis of a long learning history in which the behavior has been reinforced. As children we encountered reinforcing consequences if in the presence of a cow we said "cow." Had we said "pussycat" in the presence of a cow, we would have encountered other consequences. Consequences that influence tacting are primarily those of social interaction, as is the case generally when we learn to talk. What we say faces different consequences in the form of other people's behavior, both verbal and physical. To tact is what in everyday parlance we mean with terms like "describe," "talk about," "refer to," and so forth. That behavior analysis has coined its own term is because all these familiar words and phrases give rise to ambiguities; what is needed is a carefully defined term.

An ideal or pure tact is totally controlled by the object or event preceding it. In everyday language we would say that what is said is "correct." The social environment teaching the coming generation to talk in this way is essential to social interaction, as most clearly evidenced in situations in which the speaker tacts a phenomenon that is not immediately accessible to the listener but that makes it possible for the listener to interact with something with which he does not have direct contact. If someone sees a dog and says "dog," the response can have great significance to another person and the way this person then acts. Tacting our environment in this way is fundamental to human cooperation as it allows us to exploit the fact that "four eyes are better than two."

A given tact is triggered not only by identical objects or events. We learn to say "table" in the presence of a wide range of objects on the basis of what our social environment reinforces as correct. Objects with certain shared properties or characteristics evoke the same tact: a flat, round/rectangular/triangular surface resting on three or more "legs" triggers the tact "table." Yet in some circumstances, such as when looking for somewhere to lay out a picnic on a countryside hike, a rock might even do the same. In this way, a tact can be extended so that it may be evoked by multiple objects or events (Skinner, 1957). It is easy to see that extended tacts are very common, and pure or exact tacts really quite rare. The way in which we tact is usually inexact; however, there are areas in which we might have particular call for a pure tact, such as in science, where it is important to "know exactly what is meant."

Metaphor—a Kind of Extended Tact

Metaphors are, in Skinner's view, a form of extended tact. He cites the following example:

> "A child…upon drinking soda water for the first time, reported that it tasted 'like my foot's asleep.' The response My foot's asleep had previously been conditioned under circumstances which involved two conspicuous stimulus conditions—the partial immobility of the foot and a certain pinpoint stimulation. The property which the community used in reinforcing the response was the immobility, but the pinpoint stimulation was also important to the child. Similar stimulation, produced by drinking soda water, evoked the response" (Skinner, 1957, pp. 92–93).

In Skinner's example, the child tacts an experience that is exclusive to her, a type of event that is often called inner but that Skinner calls private. An extended tact triggered by something observable to all, such as when the presence of a certain person triggers the response "she's a terrier" can be understood in the same way. The response "a terrier" was originally learned in the presence of a particular kind of small dog and then reinforced by the social community. Something in the behavior of the person tacted in this way has a commonality with an observable property of a terrier (at least to the person who says so—the person tacting) and we end up with an extended tact. This is, in principle, the same chain of phenomena as in the above example, when a rock was tacted with the response "table."

A metaphor is thus a tact for which the triggering object or event is not the object or event that typically evokes this response in a certain linguistic community. We could look at it this way: saying "terrier" in this linguistic community has typically not been reinforced if uttered in the presence of a particular woman, and when it *is* uttered, it becomes an extended tact if evoked in her presence.

Skinner then takes the above analysis to also describe the development of a more pure or exact tact from a metaphor. If a linguistic community were to generally and continually reinforce the "terrier" tact in the presence of a person with a particular personality, the response would cease to function as a metaphor, and would be—to use a term I used earlier in this book—more "literal." Skinner describes this phenomenon as being the stabilization of an extended metaphorical tact into a more pure tact. This is what has occurred when we say that a table has legs.

Perhaps the reader has noticed that we are now in the same territory as what in both the vernacular and in linguistic metaphor research falls under the heading "dead and living metaphors" and the relationship between metaphorical and literal language. And with Skinner, as in modern linguistics, the distinction between the literal and the metaphorical is hazy, as is that between dead and living metaphors. Linguistic phenomena that at first glance seem separate on closer inspection become more overlapped. On reading Skinner, it is indeed clear that he writes at a time when literal language is taken to be axiomatically primary and the metaphorical as a sort of appendage. This seems to be axiomatic also for him. The fact that he calls a metaphor an "extended" tact suggests, I would argue, that a more pure or exact tact is primary. Skinner was writing at a time that did not know Lakoff and Johnson.

The assumption made above, that literal language is primary and the metaphorical is secondary, is gainsaid by Skinner's own analysis. A tact is nothing but operant behavior, reinforced by the linguistic community. Nothing is literal in the sense of true or objective; everything is action influenced by its consequences. Responses can thus function more or less well. What Skinner calls a pure tact is preferable if one is seeking certain consequences, while an extended tact works better in other contexts (such as when calling a rock a "table" when out hiking). And that a tact is exact rather than metaphorical is taken to be a result of learning. This would suggest that more impure—including metaphorical—tacts precede the more exact tacts in an individual's learning history; and there is no clear demarcation between the two. Skinner also writes that "a pure tact" is more of an ideal than something that actually exists in verbal behavior. Skinner's analysis thus leads to the same fundamental view of the relationship between metaphorical and literal language that we observed earlier in modern linguistics. These are two phenomena that cannot be separated other than in a crude, everyday sense. They are phenomena that exist along a continuum: living metaphors—dead metaphors—literal language. Skinner himself does not use this terminology, but writes about metaphors—extended tact—tact (albeit the other way around), but this too implies a continuum. And even if these two continuums are not simply different terms for the same thing, one detects in both views a fundamental process underlying the linguistic continuum we are discussing. We will return to the nature of this process in the next chapter when we explore the view of metaphors taken by relational frame theory. But first let me point out a few other things about Skinner's analysis and an imagined dialogue with modern linguistics over the use of metaphor.

Behavior Analysis and Linguistics— a Fruitful Union?

It is relatively easy to see that there is an overlap between what has been described with the frameworks of linguistics and Skinner's analysis, notwithstanding their different premises. If, for instance, we go by the more generally used terms in metaphor research (source and target), we find that we can apply them to Skinner's analysis. The object or the event that evoked an extended, metaphorical tact would thus be an example of the target, and the response, the tact, describes its source. If sighting a particular woman triggers the response "she's a terrier," the woman, according to current linguistic terminology, is the metaphor's target and a terrier its source; in Skinner's account of the child who said that soda tasted like "my foot's asleep," the taste sensation is the metaphor's target and the child's sensory experience of a foot going to sleep its source. If someone, when stroking the surface of a rock, says "as soft as silk," the response is, in the Skinnerian sense, an extended metaphorical tact. But in the terms I described in an earlier chapter, one would say that the surface of the rock (or the feel of it) is the metaphor's target and silk (or the sensation of what it feels like) its source.

We are thus describing a common phenomenological field from different premises and analytical perspectives, and while the points of intersection are clear, there are naturally differences as well. One important such difference is the object of our analysis. For behavior analysis it is human behavior—in this case, speech (or thinking). In more current psychological and linguistic studies, the focus is on the metaphor as a product of this speech (or thought). It is thus the content of the response that is the object of analysis. We abstract the utterance as an object in and of itself: the metaphor. One weakness with this is, of course, that we ascend to a more abstract level further away from the actual "metaphorizing." After all, metaphors are always things that are produced by actual people in actual situations.

Again, the reader might notice that the criticism thus leveled against cognitive linguistics by behavior analysis is very much echoed by many contemporary linguists, as detailed in chapter 2. Linguists like Steen (2011) and Müller (2008) stress precisely this problem, that cognitive linguistics is in danger of ignoring the concrete contexts in which metaphors are used and of focusing solely on metaphors as products of human behavior without making a close analysis of the actual process that gives rise to them. Lera Boroditsky and her team at Stanford University, as I have already discussed, are of like mind (Boroditsky, 2001; Boroditsky, Schmidt, & Phillips, 2003; Fausey & Boroditsky, 2011). Concrete language use shapes how we think and generally act, so we need to concentrate on the context in which people "metaphorize" and on the factors that influence this behavior. Metaphor use is a "cognitive process," to quote Müller again (2008, p. 17). What does this process look like? This I will be returning to in the next chapter.

The Problem Inherent to Behavior Analysis

When it comes to analyzing metaphors or metaphorical speech, behavior analysis has its own serious problem. This is most clearly illustrated by the fact that in both the heading of this section and the chapter as a whole, the implication is that behavior analysis is a uniform science, but in all my arguments I refer only to Skinner and his half-a-century-old writings. What have behavior analysts been saying about metaphor use since Skinner? Very little, if anything. Major contemporary reviews of the scientific positions of behavior analysis

(Catania, 2007) give accounts of Skinner and, to a certain extent, modern linguistics, but without developing or bringing anything new to the metaphorical table. This is part of a larger problem for behavior analysis, one that concerns how the science has moved on in its analysis of language since Skinner's days. Up until the research that engendered RFT, it has had nothing to say on metaphor use. Skinner's own ideas never inspired or informed new research and thus no deeper insights have been gained. Something was missing, not just in the understanding of metaphors but in the actual basis upon which human language is analyzed.

Conclusion

Behavior analysis was founded on the simple observation that everything we do is influenced by the circumstances in which we do it. A critical component of these circumstances is the consequences of previous actions. This applies as much to simple acts, such as picking something up from the floor, as to more complex behavior, such as writing poetry or brooding. The use of metaphorical language falls within the same frame, as behavior that is influenced by the context in which the metaphor is used. In this respect, the basic philosophy of behavior analysis has a lot to say about metaphor use more generally, and contemporary linguistics concurs with much of it. Drawing the reader's attention to these points of contact has been the purpose of this chapter. When it comes to more concrete methods of analysis we need, however, more than the theory of metaphors sketched out by Skinner over fifty years ago. We will therefore now proceed to a development of the behavior analytic approach.

CHAPTER 4

Metaphors—Relating Relations

Relational frame theory is a theory about, and a research program for, analyzing human language and cognition that has been developed over the past thirty years. The theory is based on a large number of laboratory experiments, and its fundamental principles are scientifically well supported (Hayes, Barnes-Holmes, & Roche, 2001; Dymond & Roche, 2013; Törneke, 2010; Hughes & Barnes-Holmes, 2016). Experiments designed to study metaphors and analogies on these principles have also been done (Stewart & Barnes-Holmes, 2001; Stewart, Barnes-Holmes, Roche, & Smeets, 2001; Stewart, Barnes-Holmes, & Roche, 2004; Barnes-Holmes & Stewart, 2004; Lipkens & Hayes, 2009; Ruiz & Luciano, 2011; 2015; Sierra, Ruiz, Flórez, Riaño Hernández, & Luciano, 2016). An introduction to the most important parts of the theory will help us understand how we can use it to analyze metaphors and metaphor use.

Two Fundamental Ways of Relating

To "relate" can be defined as to interact with one object in terms of another. For example, I can interact with an apple in terms of another apple, in that it is further away than another apple, larger than another apple, or redder than another apple. What I am doing is relating this apple to another. One might express the same thing by saying that I interact with the relation between two objects, in this case two apples.

All creatures interact with their surroundings in this way. Humans (and other species) are able to interact not only with a certain object (an apple, a newspaper, a tree, a cat, another human being, and so on) but also with the relation between these different objects. One coin is larger than another coin, two dogs are identical, one ball is closer than another ball, and Frank arrives just after Elisabeth.

In all these examples, the relation is dependent on the physical characteristics of the objects being related—such as color, contrast, shape, number, and size, or the position the objects take in space and time—such as one coming before the other or being closer than another. A coin is larger, two dogs have identical external features, one of two balls is geographically closer to the reactant than another, and after Elisabeth comes Frank. One could say that the immediate experience in the moment of these different objects with their individual characteristics is what determines their mutual relation. This direct means of relating can also extend over time. We can interact with an object now on the basis of the direct relation with it that was established in the past. If Frank has repeatedly arrived after Elisabeth, we can, when Elisabeth arrives, act as if Frank will also soon appear. If a bell is rung just before we are fed, we can, on hearing the bell again, act as if food will soon be made available to us. This does not apply only to us people; most other species can relate a phenomenon in the now to one that occurred earlier in their immediate experience. So we relate objects to each other on the basis of both their physical properties and our previous experience of such relations. In texts on RFT, this way of relating is often called *direct relating* and these types of relations *direct relations*.

Human beings precociously learn another way of relating, one that is principally independent of the objects' physical characteristics or properties and the position these objects take in space and time, now or in our earlier history of interacting with them. We learn to relate objects to each other through *socially approved contextual cues*, which is to say signals created by our social community. We learn, for example, to interact with a ball as "larger" not necessarily because it possesses such characteristics or properties but because of the cue—the word "larger." Imagine that I give you two balls that are physically as large as each other, one blue and the other red. I then tell you that red is bigger, and ask you which of the balls is now smaller. Or let us say that I show you two symbols, ϕ and Δ. I tell you that Δ is 10,000 US dollars and that ϕ *is twice as much as* Δ. Which of the two would you rather have?

When answering questions like this (the blue one is smaller; I want ϕ), we do so by relating the objects or phenomena that the questions ask us about. But we are not relating the objects merely in terms of some inherent property or necessarily out of our previous experience of them, but on the bases of other contextual cues (words, gestures). ϕ is not inherently worth 20,000 dollars and the blue ball is not physically smaller than the red one. None of us needs previous experience of the two symbols or of the two colored balls. We are playing a shared game that can be said to "move around" properties between objects and events and this "moving around" is done by relating objects on the basis of arbitrary contextual cues, such as "smaller," "larger," and "twice as much." In saying arbitrary, I mean that the cues have a social origin, and have emerged as common praxis through human interaction. Relating on the basis of cues like these is principally different to the first type of relating I described based on the properties or characteristics of objects, or their position in time and space.

These types of *indirect relations* that we thus create are what we normally call symbolic, and what enables human "symbolization." The technical term used in RFT for this type of relating is *arbitrarily applicable relational responding*, implying its nature as a response (a behavior), or something done by one or more people. That it is a relational response simply means that the behavior is a type of relating. And that the responding is arbitrarily applicable means that since it is controlled by arbitrary contextual cues it can be applied to anything. We humans can relate anything to anything in any possible way. Another term for the same behavior is to *frame relationally*, hence the term *relational frame theory*.

This ability to relate objects and phenomena through arbitrary contextual cues is, according to RFT, the very basis of human language. It is thus not to be understood as a consequence of language but as its *fundamental building block*. It is learning to do this that lies at the heart of infant language acquisition, and it is when we have learned to do this that we can speak with meaning and listen with understanding.

Different Relational Frames

When we generally talk about the faculty of symbolization, we are primarily referring to a kind of relationship whereby one thing stands for or represents another. The word "car" represents an actual car, the word "parsnip" an actual vegetable, and the name "Per" an actual person. In RFT, this kind of relation is called a *relation of coordination* and is the most fundamental relational frame.

But we can also relate objects in many other ways by making use of different *relational frames*. All the relations with which we interact on the basis of the intrinsic properties of objects, or on the position they take in space and time, can also be established via arbitrary contextual cues. We can interact with a branch of a tree through its direct relations (its being part of the tree) but we also relate to another person on the basis of the indirect relation that he is "one of us beginners." In both cases, there is what is called a *hierarchical relation*, by which is meant that something is a component or part of something else—in the former instance a direct relation depending on the tree's intrinsic properties, in the latter an indirect relation established via relational framing. We can interact with a person as being physically larger than another, and we can interact with a person as a greater author than another. This is a *comparative relation*, in the first case a direct such, and in the second an indirect. We can interact with Elisabeth coming through the door immediately after Frank as this happens and we can interact with the fact that "Frank will arrive after Elisabeth tomorrow," where the first example is a *temporal relation* of a direct kind, and the second a temporal relation established via relational framing (what we have been calling an indirect relation). The so-called future ("tomorrow") is only contactable via arbitrary cues, never via direct experience.

Using relational framing, we give things around us properties that they do not have through their physical characteristics and without us having any direct experience of them. A comic amongst others can be "a rarity," a shirt can be "fashionable," and a dish "dangerous to eat" even though we have never eaten it before and it smells delicious. The way we frame events and objects relationally governs how different things influence our behavior and this is the crux of its significance for us. The way we relate *transforms* our environment's influence on us. Things can be desirable or necessary to avoid, not only because of their intrinsic properties or our previous experience of them, but because of how we relate them to other things under the influence of arbitrary contextual cues. If you have had contact with Bill and found the experience unnerving, and then someone says that "Lars is just like Bill," you might want to avoid Lars even if you have never met him and thus have no direct experience of what he is like as a person. You react on the basis of how you relate Lars to Bill (and on your experience with Bill). And this relating takes place through a socially learned, and essentially arbitrary, game.

A separate type of relational frame that is thought to be very important to us, our behavior, and our self-experience is that known as *deictic framing*.[3] This refers to how we can establish and act from a certain perspective, and to how this perspective can vary. He said so *then*, establishes when it was said. *Then* denotes a perspective that is different from *now*. *Here* is another perspective, as opposed to *there*. *I* is a perspective that is different from the perspective of *you*. We can relate to something *now* on the basis of what we think will happen *then*, and I can do something on the basis of what *I* think that *you* or *she* will do if *I* act in a certain way. This perspective-taking is a type of relational framing. In technical terms, this is an example of arbitrarily applicable relational responses. And these responses occur under the influence of arbitrary social cues. Therefore we can also "switch perspective" and answer questions like: "If you were me, what would your surname be?" and "If you were in Portugal, what ocean would be to your west?"

Deictic framing seems to be particularly crucial to our experience of continuity over time and space. We experience that we "are the same person" in some sense, regardless of change. If I were to ask you to call to mind an actual activity in which you were engaged last summer and then ask you if you are certain that *you* were the one doing it, you would think it odd. Your experience of "it was me" who was there last summer would probably be quite unequivocal. The same would apply if I asked you to recall an event from your teens or even from when before you started school. You would naturally observe that the person you refer to as "I" has changed in many ways: in how you look, in how you think about yourself and others, and so forth. And yet you experience that "it was me" in some sense. The person who was there then and called themselves "I" is the same "I" who is now remembering all this. This seems to be more a profoundly fundamental experiential aspect of being human than any kind of logical conclusion as such. The same would be true if I were to ask you to remember a situation in which your emotional state was totally different from what it is now as you read these lines—one of elation, perhaps, or of deep despair. And at the same time, that sense of "it was me" is there as well.

This experience of continuity is assumed to be a consequence of how we have been trained, almost from the moment we start verbalizing, to talk about

---

3   This is a linguistic term derived from the Greek deixis (demonstration) that is used to denote words or expressions that refer to the position or perspective from which something happens, such as place (here), time (then) and agent (she).

and gradually experience the perspective that one could encapsulate as I-here-now, that unique perspective from which each and every one of us observes and otherwise interacts with our environment. It is a combination of different deictic frames, spatial (here/there) and temporal (now/then). Everything we experience we experience from "I-here-now."

This perspective is also a vantage point from which to observe ourselves. So, for instance, we can observe that we have changed since childhood, we can observe that we think different things, remember one thing one moment and another thing the next, and note that we can feel different things. But the experience of being simultaneously the one who has been and who is constantly there noticing "myself" and the continuity this implies is at the heart of the human experience. Since this perspective, which is unique to every individual, has arisen as a result of deictic framing, it is often called the "deictic I." This type of relational framing of phenomena occurring "within ourselves" (our own thoughts, feelings, memories, physical sensations) is combined with hierarchical framing (one thing being a part of another) to become a central aspect of our ability to interact with our own behavior, with ourselves (Luciano, Valdivia-Salas, Cabello-Luque, & Hernández, 2009). We will be returning to this in the book's clinical section, since the way we interact with ourselves, according to RFT, is critical to flexible human behavior in general. Here there is a key to understanding psychological problems and to influencing them.

The above was an attempt to summarize the substance of relational frame theory in a way that will help us tackle the main theme of this book: metaphors and how they operate. Readers who wish to learn more about RFT and the science behind it would do well to read other overviews (Dymond & Roche, 2013; Hughes & Barnes-Holmes, 2016; Törneke, 2010), which also contain specific references to basic research.

Relational Framing and Metaphors

Relational framing is thus a skill we learn from an early age that consists of being able to relate objects independently of their intrinsic properties and our immediate experience of these objects. This relating is controlled by arbitrary contextual cues, such as sound combinations (words) and gestures. In the rudimentary case we relate two objects on the basis of such cues: one thing "is bigger than" another, "comes later than" another, "is the same as" another, "is part of" another, "is underneath" another, or "is seen from there." But much more complex phenomena can also be related in this way. For instance, the type of phenomenon we generally call "an experience" can be coordinated with something of which we have no experience but that comes "later" (a contextual cue for temporal framing) and we can act as if "a similar experience can recur." We can also, however, establish another type of relation between these experiences, such as "a similar experience *cannot* recur" (in other words, a relating that places the experience in contrary relation to what might happen in the future). It is easy to see how the "properties" with which we thus endow the future can influence how we act. Exceedingly complex phenomena in the past (World War II) can be juxtaposed with something equally complex happening now (a specific political event) and what might happen in the future: "What's happening now in central Europe is like the run-up to the second world war—we must make sure to turn the trend."

Complex phenomena are those that in themselves comprise a nexus of relations. Historical events (such as World War II or current events in Central Europe) contain relations of similarity, dissimilarity, time, compositeness (hierarchy), and so forth. The same applies to private experiences. The experience of talking to a neighbor contains relations between what I said, what she said, where we both stood, differences and similarities, to name but a few. And if I compare this conversation to one that I have seen in a film, I relate two complex phenomena each of which comprises a number of different relations. When we relate different complex phenomena with each other, we are thus relating relations.

According to RFT, this is at the very heart of understanding what we do when we use analogies and metaphors: *We relate relations*. Since the relations we relate are often composed of several other relations (such as in the example of different historical events), we can say that we relate relational networks.[4] Let me give you some clear and relatively simple examples to illustrate the basic principle:

Peter and Louise are like two peas in a pod. Peas (this analogy's source) have a certain intrinsic relation. In an expression such as this, the intended relation is presumably one of similarity. This is a nonarbitrary (direct) relation based on the physical properties of peas. The relation that the listener of the analogy

---

4   Note that the term relational network makes no reference to any existing object but to our ability to relate in complex ways.

already knows from the analogy's source is now established for its target: Peter and Louise. This occurs via an arbitrary contextual signal in the form of "*are like*" and a coordination relation between two peas on the one hand and the relation between Peter and Louise on the other is established (see figure 4.1). In most cases, the arbitrarily established relation used in analogies and metaphors is a coordination relation. A certain relation (the one between two peas) is equated to, or coordinated with, another relation (that between Peter and Louise). The relations that form part of the relational networks related to can, however, vary in kind. In this example, it is a relation of similarity (between two peas), but a number of different relations can, in this way, be established for the analogy's or metaphor's target. Take the following example: *Peter and Louise are like night and day.* Again, two relations are coordinated (that between night and day on the one hand, and between Peter and Louise on the other.) Here, the metaphor's source contains a relation of dissimilarity, possibly even opposition—and that is the relation that is established between Peter and Louise (see figure 4.2). A third example is: *Peter and Louise are like cats and dogs.* Here, the nexus of relations that form the metaphor's source is a more

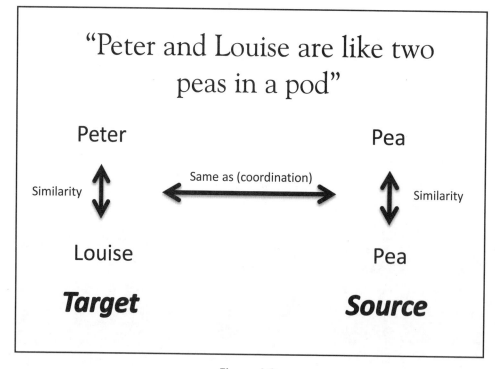

Figure 4.1

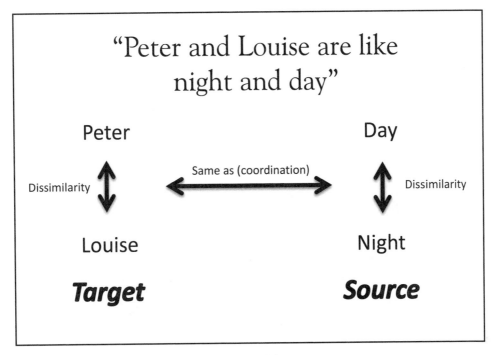

Figure 4.2

complex relational network, which we could summarize with the phrase "relation of conflict" or the like (see figure 4.3).

Another example: A man acts hesitantly and evasively at the thought of doing something he really wants to do, like approach an attractive person. An observer might say: "He's like a cat around hot cream." Two phenomena are related here: a man's hesitant dithering (the metaphor's target) and how a cat might conceivably act when wanting food but also not wanting to burn itself (the metaphor's source).

This occurs via an arbitrary contextual signal, *like*, and thus the established coordination relation is arbitrary or indirect. Each of the two related phenomena is composed of a network of relations, many of which are direct (relations between different aspects of the phenomena in question based on their respective characteristics). The two phenomena related in this example encompass temporal relations (certain things precede others) and spatial relations (distance/proximity), among others. All in all, we can describe the relations within each network as "acting avoidant" (See figure 4.4).

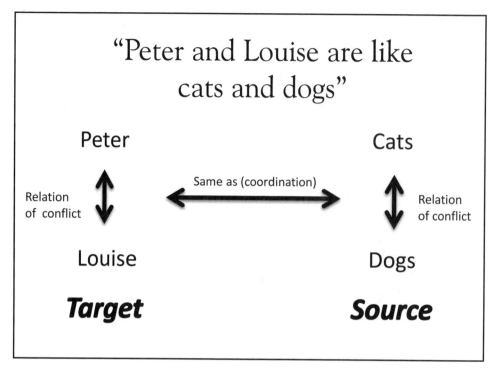

Figure 4.3

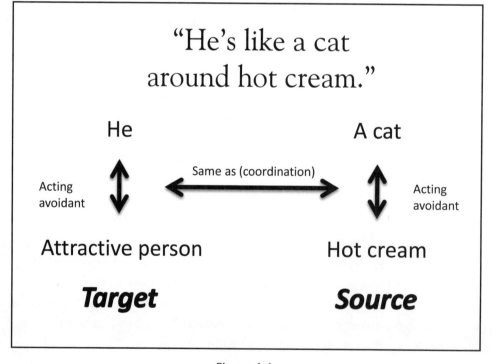

Figure 4.4

The Importance of Direct Relations

Metaphors thus consist not only of indirect (arbitrary) relations established via arbitrary contextual cues, but also of direct (nonarbitrary) relations, relations that have a pivotal function. Consider the examples above in which different metaphorical expressions were employed to describe how Peter and Louise relate to each other. The source of these different metaphors (the relation between two peas, between night and day, and between cats and dogs) has certain characteristics, and it is when these characteristics can also be noted in the target (the relation between Peter and Louise) that the metaphor is deemed pertinent. In a well-functioning metaphor, the source has a higher degree of such characteristics than the target. Two peas are more alike than Peter and Louise, but there is also a similarity between the latter, and herein lies the power of the metaphor. Night and day are more dissimilar than Peter and Louise, but it is the differences between them that give the metaphor meaning. The same is true when the relation between cats and dogs serves as the source. If you fail to see any kind of conflict between Peter and Louise, you would probably say that the metaphor is inappropriate; however, if you can see such a conflict, regardless of how subtle, the source clarifies or focuses these characteristics in the target. The following is thus needed to create a metaphor:

1. Two relational networks.

2. A coordination relation between these two networks.

3. A relational network forming the source of the metaphor which has an aspect/direct relation/property of a more salient or obvious nature than the corresponding aspect/direct relation/property in the relational network forming the target of the metaphor.

4. Thereby the significance or function of the target is changed.

If someone says of Alexander that "he's a big teddy bear," then "teddy bear" is the relational network that constitutes the metaphor's source, and the aspects or properties that are central to the metaphor are more pronounced or noticeable in teddy bears than they are in Alexander, the metaphor's target. But for the metaphor to be pertinent, the listener must be able to identify these properties in Alexander as well. These properties may already be visible to the listener, in which case the metaphor clarifies or focuses them, makes them "stand out" in Alexander. Sometimes, however, these characteristics in the metaphor's target only become manifest to the listener when the metaphor is uttered. It is as if the properties of the relational network that constitutes the metaphor's target are "uncovered" by the metaphor. When the metaphor has this effect, it is experienced as especially striking or apt. It says something new. Take, for example, "Awakening is a parachute jump from the dream" (Tranströmer, 2011). I would guess that for most readers this is one such innovative likeness. The relational network that makes up the metaphor's source (a parachute jump) has certain properties that we can also recognize in its target (waking up from a dream), but we do so only once we have been exposed to the metaphor.

A good metaphor is thus unidirectional, since the property upon which it rides is more salient in the source. One might say of two peas that they are like Peter and Louise (if they are clearly similar) but the metaphor is a poor one since Peter and Louise's similarity adds almost nothing to that of the two peas (which is more salient). One might say of a teddy bear that it is like Alexander, but the statement is experienced as saying little about the bear since the properties referred to are more marked in it than in Alexander.

This unidirectionality of a typical metaphor distinguishes it from a classic analogy, which is more bidirectional. Take "an atom is like the solar system." This analogy is normally used in such a way that the solar system (which is assumed to be better known) serves as the analogy's source and the atom as its target. But the property referred to (the spatial relation of smaller objects orbiting a larger one) is just as pronounced in both, and if someone is familiar with this simplified model of the atom but not the solar system, she could use the atom as the source and the solar system as the target and say that "the solar system is like an atom." An analogy such as "Mercedes and BMWs are like apples and pears" is also quite typical. The properties referred to (they are both items in a general class of either cars or fruit) are as pronounced in both source and target and can therefore be inverted, so it would be equally meaningful to say that "apples and pears are like Mercedes and BMWs." This would work much better than if one tried to invert a typical metaphor, such as Peter and Louise are like two peas in a pod. The metaphor is unidirectional, since the relevant aspect, property, or direct relation is more salient in the metaphor's source than in its target.

Relational Frame Theory and Modern Linguistics

In RFT, metaphor use is thus seen as a variant of the fundamental linguistic repertoire: to relate phenomena on the basis of arbitrary contextual cues. Source and target consist of more or less complex relational networks that are related through arbitrary contextual cues. This analysis is very similar to what is being propounded by contemporary linguists specializing in metaphor use, particularly Cornelia Müller, whose contributions I have already discussed (Müller, 2008). Even though she describes the phenomenon from scientific premises other than behavior analysis, her account does have some striking similarities. She stresses the importance of analyzing the very action of establishing a metaphor in a given historical context and how metaphor use comprises a "triad" (her term) consisting of what is classically referred to as the metaphor's source and target, plus another ingredient that establishes the metaphorical expression. She writes: "There is an entity or process A, which relates two entities B and C, such that C is seen in terms of B" (Müller, 2008, p. 30). She thus describes two domains that are linked by a verbal (cognitive) act. This cognitive process is, according to RFT, the coordination of two networks of relations on the basis of an arbitrary contextual cue. RFT thus offers a research program with well-operationalized terms that are potentially very fruitful for linguists researching metaphors, especially given that RFT has a contextual premise and potential tools for predicting and influencing concrete metaphorizing in a given experimental situation. RFT, for its part, could draw much material from this extensive research field to test against. A potentially fascinating collaboration might be within reach.

Metaphors and Deictic Framing

As I discussed in the previous section on different types of relational frames, deictic framing—the ability to adopt different perspectives according to arbitrary cues—is a critical learned skill, and one that plays an important part in our use of metaphors. Consider the "she's a terrier" example. Ostensibly, such an utterance relates solely to a particular woman and a particular breed of dog. On closer inspection, however, the referent is not just these two beings but also an "implicit third," a person who is assumed to interact with them. The metaphor does not say primarily how these two (Eva and the terrier) relate mutually to each other, but how they are similar if one (a third person, possibly the one hearing the metaphor) interacts with them. If one were to express the metaphor more fully or explain exactly what is related to what, one might say: "Interacting with Eva is like interacting with a terrier." It is the possible consequences of interacting with Eva that resemble the consequences of interacting with a terrier—a similarity that is established via the arbitrary cue *like*. The presence of an "implicit third" is usually not expressed in metaphorical speech. But it is only when one assumes the existence of a listener (or another person, someone with a perspective, who is the observer) that the utterance works. And this assumption is shared by two people in dialogue, since the faculty required to experience oneself as a speaker to a listener (and as the listener to a speaker) is part of our verbal or linguistic competence. Being an "I" and experiencing the existence of a "you" and a "he/she" is established for us when we learn deictic framing and is often built into metaphorical speech, even when it is not made explicit. This also applies, for example, to the metaphor that Tomas Tranströmer uses when he equates a parachute jump with awakening from a dream. A person who wakes up and a person doing a parachute jump are assumed givens. The same applies to a great many of the so-called conceptual metaphors described in the first chapter. Metaphors like "life is a journey," "ideas are food," "argument is war," and "anger is pressure contained" presuppose a person who travels, eats, argues, fights, and gets angry. Metaphorical speech usually makes use of deictic framing, so that the speaker speaks according to her own and other perspectives with the assumption that her listener shares that experience. This insight makes it clearer that metaphors are about relating relations, even when what is related to what is not explicitly and fully included in the metaphorical expression.

Causal Relations Are Often Central

So what relations are then related in these more complex metaphors? What we are dealing with is relational networks composed of multiple relations, and to ascertain which ones are crucial to any given example we usually need to know the context in which the utterance is spoken. The meaning of a metaphor is not independent of its context. Quite the contrary: its meaning is contextually dependent. There are factors other than the mere words used that determine how both listener and speaker relate, and the "meaning" with which a metaphor is endowed. This is taken as read from a behavior analytic perspective, but the opinion is shared by many contemporary linguists, as I mentioned in chapter 2.

Let us return to the "she's a terrier" metaphor. We assume that the metaphor is spoken when the woman, whom we may call Eva, gives as good as she gets in a discussion and refuses to back down from her opinion despite the efforts of someone else to ignore or contradict it. It is the consequences of someone's interaction with a terrier and with Eva that is the crux of the metaphor. This central aspect of the metaphor is initially more marked on the interaction with a terrier (its source) but is clarified (or discovered) as an aspect of the interaction with Eva (its target) as the utterance is spoken. In this situation, we may describe the significance of the metaphor as "the consequences of taking on Eva are like the consequences of taking on a terrier." In this case, the consequences can be described as the experience of fierce resistance (see figure 4.5). Someone who has never met Eva might benefit greatly in some way from this information, which might influence how he will then act in relation to Eva.

That metaphors are often used to influence both one's own behavior and that of other people is presumably the reason why causal relations are so

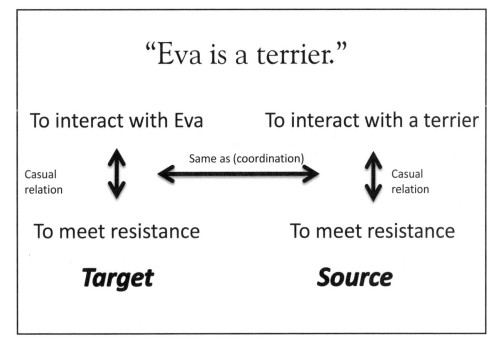

Figure 4.5

common in the relational networks that are related in many metaphors. To influence is to bring about an effect, to achieve consequences. This is a fundamental aspect of behavior, and thus also central to language. The ability to say (and think) something that makes the desired consequences more likely is essential to the survival of both the individual and the group. Metaphors that function in this way can therefore be said to constitute rules, advice, or instructions for action. If so, the metaphor describes the connection between actions and their possible consequences. The capacity to understand and follow instructions is taken to be the most important consequence of language (Catania, 2007), and metaphor use is a subset of this repertoire. So metaphors that we "live by," to paraphrase Lakoff and Johnson, (see chapter 1) are often those that describe the consequences of actions; in other words, causal relations are critical to the phenomena being related. Some more examples:

Someone who has just finished work for the day says to a colleague still sitting at her desk working, "If you carry on like this you'll hit the wall." The consequences of working too hard are placed in a coordination relation with the consequences of "hitting a wall" (see figure 4.6). A soccer team is up at halftime in a crucial match, and as the players leave the dressing room for the

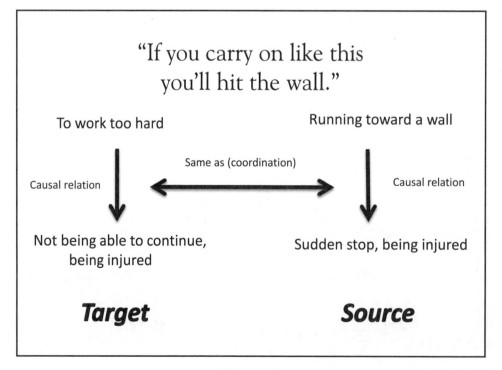

Figure 4.6

second half the coach says: "Now you get out there and seal the deal!" The consequences of playing in a certain way are equated with the consequences of "sealing a deal" (see figure 4.7).

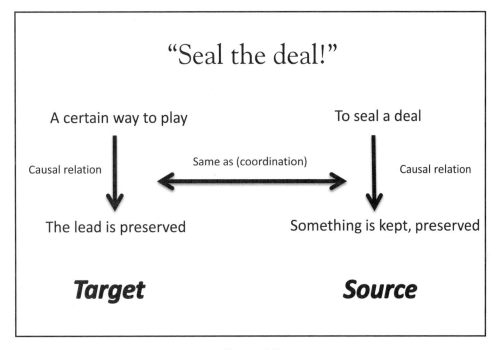

Figure 4.7

Conclusion

According to relational frame theory, a certain behavioral repertoire is the bedrock of language: the ability to relate phenomena based on arbitrary contextual cues rather than on mere physical properties and the direct experience of a relation between them. In consequence, we can, in theory, relate anything to anything in any possible way. This skill explains how metaphors work: by relating relations. A metaphor comprises two relational networks juxtaposed in a coordination relation, where the network that provides the metaphor's source has a property or an aspect that is more salient than it is in the network that provides its target. Metaphor use is an essential part of verbal behavior and is used to influence how we interact with other people and our physical milieu.

CHAPTER 5

Metaphors in Clinical Research

As pointed out in the introduction, different schools of psychotherapy are in agreement about how useful metaphors are, although many questions on why and how are still unanswered—at least if one wants a scientific answer. Questions concerning the relationship between metaphor use and treatment outcomes have been particularly tricky (McMullen, 2008). However, despite the lack of studies comparing and mutually evaluating different types of intervention, the research field is not barren, and there are a number of studies charting metaphor use in concrete therapeutic situations that attempt to draw conclusions on essential variables, most of them conducted by researchers and therapists working with a psychodynamic or emotional processing (e.g. Greenberg & Pavio, 1997) model.

The majority of these studies follow the same kind of pattern: you choose some concrete treatments, either ongoing or especially initiated, and then follow either a partial or a full course of therapy, recording the interaction between therapist and client. This you then use to code metaphor use in the dialogue in some way so that you can concentrate on either the therapist's or the client's use of metaphors—or indeed both, as in the case of many later studies. Variables under study can be the number of metaphors used, who initiates a particular metaphor, whether this metaphor is developed, who uses most metaphors, recurrent themes, and so forth. In some studies, this provides the material with which the overall therapeutic outcome and/or other metrics are correlated. Some studies have another stage of data collection, whereby the researchers select specific sequences from the recorded therapeutic sessions that are judged to be of interest to a particular point of inquiry, show them to the therapist and client, and ask them about how they experienced them at the time and how they rate their significance. This material is then used in an attempt to find correlations between aspects of metaphor use and outcome or process variables. The studies normally include a small number of cases (three to six), although some are much larger (McMullen & Convey, 2002).

What conclusions can be drawn from these studies? As the researchers themselves often point out, the conclusions are unreliable owing to the size of the studies. There are, however, some findings that are lent some validity by their recurrence, especially when they agree with what we generally know about metaphor use from the research I have referred to above.

- The number of metaphors used in therapy does not seem to be an important marker of efficacy (Angus, 1996). There are some studies in which the total number of metaphors used by either the therapist or the client correlates with what, in terms of other variables, can be assumed to be good outcomes, although other studies show the opposite (McMullen, 2008). The hypothesis that the number of metaphors used per se should predict effective therapy also seems to contradict what we more generally know about metaphors and their linguistic function. Metaphors are not a specialist linguistic tool that can be said to be helpful or not helpful, but are the very building blocks of language in general. The more we talk, the more metaphors we use (Angus & Korman, 2002). It is therefore reasonable to expect all ways of speaking and thinking, be they constructive or destructive, to be infused with metaphors. This seems also to coincide with what we see in clinical research.

- One type of metaphor use that seems to correlate with positive outcome and/or process metrics is one of cooperation between therapist and client (Angus, 1996; Angus & Rennie, 1988; 1989). These are metaphors that, after having been introduced into the dialogue, are "cocreated" (developed and used) by both. It does not seem to matter so much who initiated such helpful metaphors. These findings also correspond with what we know in general about therapist-client cooperation, particularly with regard to treatment goals, as a positive marker of therapeutic efficacy (Tryon & Winograd, 2011).

- The metaphors used by a client often contain themes that are central to the client's problem (Levitt, Korman, & Angus, 2000;

Angus & Korman, 2002; McMullen, 2008). This suggests that therapists should make every effort to explore the metaphors the clients use, their associations and implicit content, and to use this material in their continuing dialogue. This conclusion also agrees with the idea of metaphors being the bedrock of language. "The mouth speaks what the heart is full of" even when the speech is metaphorical. It might even be the case that our words are especially "from the heart" when we use metaphors.

- The difference between "dead" and "living" metaphors appears unimportant with regard to finding central metaphors in a therapeutic situation. Even those that would be seen as dead or petrified can prove essential as much to understanding as to change (McMullen, 1989; Rasmussen & Angus, 1996). In this respect too, the conclusions tally with what contemporary linguists have been writing more generally about metaphors (Müller, 2008).

- Overarching metaphorical themes can provide the frame within which successful change conversations can be held (McMullen, 1989; Angus, 1996). When effective therapies are compared with less successful ones in these studies, researchers find that the former are marked by a central "metaphorical theme" that is developed as therapy progresses and that recurs via individual metaphors connected to this theme. The change in the client's problem is also reflected in her mode of speech within the frame of the metaphorical theme. If, for example, the client has initially described herself as being "trapped in a corner," she might later talk about the ability to "move more freely." If another client has initially described himself as "at war" with his wife, at the end of a successful course of therapy he might describe himself as having "made peace" with her, or state that the war "is being won." Again, we note that these findings agree with what linguists would say are the mechanisms of metaphorical speech.

- If the therapist deliberately uses metaphors, it increases the chances that the client will remember what the therapist has said (Martin, Cummings, & Hallberg, 1992).

Linguists Study Psychotherapy

In recent years, linguists have also taken an interest in how metaphors are used in psychotherapy (Needham-Didsbury, 2014; Tay, 2013; 2016a; 2016b; Tay & Jordan, 2015). Given their lack of attention to the effects of psychotherapy, their research and analyses are not clinical in the classical sense, yet they still fall under this heading as they are devoted to actual clinical interaction. These linguists look at the psychotherapeutic function of metaphors from the premise that I described in chapter 2, namely that metaphors are to be understood in terms of the context in which they are used, the therapeutic interaction being one such context. The studies and the analyses are chiefly qualitative and attempt to interrogate clinical interaction from the point of modern linguistic metaphor theory. An ambitious example of this is Dennis Tay's book *Metaphor in Psychotherapy: A Descriptive and Prescriptive Analysis* (2013), in which he uses transcriptions from actual therapeutic sessions to explore different aspects of the verbal interaction. The following points are conclusions based mainly on his work.

- The sources used in metaphorical speech in typical therapeutic dialogues can be divided into embodied, cultural, and individual-specific. That our bodies and our physical interaction with our surroundings are common sources of metaphorical speech is also true of metaphors in psychotherapy. Cultural and individual aspects are also often evident. If someone says of the atmosphere at a meeting that it was "as hot as a car park in Bangkok," it is obvious that a physical experience of heat is the source of the metaphorical expression, but also that a personal experience of Thailand's capital city probably is.

- Metaphors often serve as "conceptual pacts" in problem solving (Brennan & Clark, 1996). A metaphor is introduced by one dialogue partner and is subsequently processed by both therapist and client to become a key component of their shared mode of expression within which a problem or difficulty, and a solution or means of acting are formulated.

- Just as much as one can trace continuity of metaphor use in a psychotherapeutic dialogue, one may also observe a degree of variability. Continuity is typically manifest when both therapist and client resort to the same source for the same target. For example, they might constantly refer to the client's relationship with his wife as "a war," talking about how they fight their battles, who attacks first, and so forth; here, they make repeated use of a given source (war) for the same target (the client's relationship), and together develop the metaphor. If one of them uses a previously used source for a different target, similarity is established between different aspects of experience or behavior. For example, if the client has previously spoken of his relationship in terms of a war and then says when discussing his job, "I'm at war there too," we see that the source (war) is applied to a new target (his job). It is also common for different sources to be used for one and the same target. An example of this would be saying, after having frequently talked about the client's relationship in terms of a war, that they have "reached a crossroads." The relationship is still the target, but the source has shifted from a "war" to a "journey." Such a discursive event can give a fresh perspective or modify the description of a phenomenon (in this case a relationship) and provide new opportunities for progress. A frequent chopping and changing of both source and target indicates a problem in the dialogue.

- Metaphors are not only a feature of psychotherapeutic discourse; they also influence us when we talk about the therapy itself. If we describe the therapy as a journey, as a collaborative project, as a chance for someone to get things off her chest, as a way of acquiring tools, as a means of processing emotions or coming to terms with the past, it implies a number of different things about how both therapist and client actually behave in the therapeutic situation.

Research Shortcomings

As pointed out at the start of the chapter, there are many questions one may ask in clinical research to which there are no clear answers. The gap between clinical practice and basic research on metaphor has also been recognized for a long time by clinicians and researchers in the empirical tradition (McCurry & Hayes, 1992; Stott et al. 2010). Some researchers say that this is not simply because the field is too complex or the number of clinical studies too small, but because the approach commonly used is itself encumbered with quite a few principle difficulties. This argument is put most cogently by Linda McMullen in an essay synopsizing the subject (McMullen, 2008). The conclusions she draws are of particular interest to anyone approaching the subject from a behavior analytic point of view. Even though she makes no reference to this branch of psychology, what she writes coincides closely with its assumptions. She starts by noting that different studies often use different definitions of key phenomena and that this makes it hard to construct a knowledge base and replicate findings. Clearer definitions are thus called for. She also argues that clinical research has not taken sufficient account of actual metaphor use and the context in which it occurs: hence the title of her essay, "Putting It in Context." She contests that focus on metaphors per se can be a mistake, and that this is associated with a view of language as context-independent, and advocates a more functional approach to language, emphasizing its "strategic use [which] requires that we focus on what talk between a speaker and a listener in a particular context is *accomplishing*" (McMullen, 2008 p. 408, my italics). Instead of focusing on metaphor use in general, she says, this approach would lead us to a primary interest in clinically relevant phenomena, and only then in how metaphors operate in these very contexts.

Linguist Dennis Tay also points out that existing research on metaphor use suffers from a lack of shared definitions (Tay, 2013), and notes that scholars with a primary interest in psychotherapy are often ignorant of the advances being made in linguistic research and metaphor theory. At the same time, he points to the lack of knowledge about psychotherapy research in his own scientific field, calls for cooperation, and suggests ways that this could be accomplished (Tay, 2014; 2016c).

Conclusion

Clinical research on the use of metaphors leaves many unanswered questions, particularly with regard to the link between particular metaphor use and specific therapeutic outcomes. The studies that have been conducted show, however, that metaphorical language is common in psychotherapy, and that key themes in both problem-describing and solution-attempting are often dressed as metaphors. This is also what one would expect, given the pervasiveness of metaphors in general.

Some tentative conclusions can, however, be drawn from the research available. It does not seem as if the significant aspect of therapeutic dialogue is the number of metaphors used but the collaboration between therapist and client on formulating those relating to key themes. The classic distinction between dead and living metaphors also does not seem to have any crucial relevance, an example of how what we know about metaphor function in language and thought, especially from linguistic research, is also applicable to psychotherapy. This is also confirmed by linguists who, on dissecting actual therapeutic dialogues, also draw the conclusion that the ability to cooperate and jointly formulate key thematic metaphors is crucial to psychotherapy. I will be returning to this idea in the book's clinical section.

CHAPTER 6

What Have We Learned?

In this brief chapter, I will be summarizing the main conclusions of my review of contemporary metaphor research, and in so doing offering a shortcut for readers uninterested in familiarizing themselves with the deeper levels of scholarly research and theory. They can read this chapter for an overview of chapters 1 to 5, and go straight to clinical application, although I hope that they will be enticed back to gain a more thorough grasp of the issues at hand. But this is, of course, entirely up to them. The following points sum up what I think modern science tells us about metaphors and their use:

- Metaphors are not "linguistic ornamentation" or appendages to more literal language, but a fundamental building block of language.

- The way we use language every day betrays the fact that we constantly use metaphors in the way we interact with our surroundings, with each other, and with ourselves—even when we are not aware that we are doing so. We "look forward" to the summer, "we incline toward" wanting to go away for the weekend, and we either "buy" what someone tells us or "brush it aside." We "boil" with anger and "freeze" in terror.

- To metaphorize is to talk about one thing in terms of another, and is what we do when describing a more unfamiliar, unclear, or abstract phenomenon (the metaphor's target) with reference to one that is more familiar, clear, or concrete (the metaphor's source).

- Metaphor use is a highly potent instrument for influencing human behavior in general.

- The traditional classification of language into literal and metaphorical/figurative has very little to offer other than in a crude, everyday sense.

- The classification of metaphors into living and dead is not clear-cut either. Dead metaphors are often revived in dialogue, and can exert considerable influence on both the speaker and the listener.

- Metaphors are always uttered in a context. If we are to understand metaphor use, we must always analyze them in the contexts in which they are used.

- The tenets of behavior analysis tally in many ways with modern trends in the linguistic analysis of metaphor use. Metaphorizing is behavior that is to be understood functionally—in other words, in terms of the effects it has on the listener.

- The behavioral repertoire at the heart of language in general is also at the heart of metaphor use. "Languaging" is a special way of relating: it is to frame relationally. Relational frame theory offers a definition of what we do when we metaphorize: we relate relations.

- Metaphor use is very common in psychotherapeutic dialogue, and overarching metaphorical themes often comprise the frame within which change conversations can be effectively held.

- The degree of cooperation between therapist and client with regard to the use and development of metaphors seems to be a prognostic factor in psychotherapy.

PART 2

Metaphors as Therapeutic Tools

CHAPTER 7

Three Core Strategies

This chapter takes as its starting point the conclusion that Linda McMullen draws in her summary review of the research being conducted into metaphor use in psychotherapy (McMullen, 2008). She writes: "One way to begin thinking about what a contextual approach would entail is to start not with a focus on metaphors, per se, but rather on events of clinical interest …" (p. 408). She develops her ideas by stressing the specific function that metaphor use can conceivably have in a given therapeutic dialogue. To use a metaphor is an act, and to understand its point we must take an interest in the consequences this metaphor has in the context in which it is uttered.

Areas of Clinical Interest

So what are the events of clinical interest on which we have reason to focus? Finding the answer to this question is the intention of this chapter. My opening tactic is to widen the scope of my search. Which areas are emphasized by the evidence-based psychological therapeutic models? Is there, amongst these models, any consensus on where one should look? To some extent I think there is, and I shall start by describing seven such areas on the basis of current psychotherapeutic models that are empirically supported: motivation, psychoeducation, thinking, exposure, emotional processing, relationship, and proaction. While these different areas are not well defined, nor clearly demarcated from each other, they will have to serve here as the departure point for a search for more fundamental principles. I will later argue that Relational Frame Theory (RFT) can be used to describe key aspects of psychological problems and the clinical processes on which we are to focus. RFT can be used to analyze different aspects of clinical interventions (Törneke, 2010; Villatte, Villatte, & Hayes,

2016). Here I will use RFT to sum up the areas of consensus described by different evidence-based models of psychotherapy, and formulate three basic psychotherapeutic strategies, which can then provide guidelines for how to use metaphors in our efforts to help people toward change. Focus will be on the way we interact with our own behavior. But let us, as I said, start by casting our net wide.

Motivation

Motivation is taken to be a crucial variable in different types of psychotherapy. Either as a therapeutic prerequisite (Craske & Barlow, 2014; Franklin & Foa, 2014) or as a specific area of therapeutic focus (Payne, Ellard, Farchione, Fairholme, & Barlow, 2014). One model that places particular stress on interventions contrived to target this phenomenological area is motivational interviewing (MI) (Miller & Rollnick, 2013). This interview method has its roots in drug rehabilitation, but has general application (Lundahl & Burke, 2009). Few other models of psychological counseling have devoted so much research to understanding which aspects of a therapist's approach facilitate change (Miller & Rose, 2009). The idea is that in MI the therapist, by engaging in empathetic, reflective dialogue, helps the client to explore his[5] own reason for change, and that the client's own emergent formulation of a personal will and ability to effect change makes it more likely that the change will actually happen. This way of talking, about wanting and being able to change ("change talk") predicts change. Much of the research has been dedicated to examining how the client's way of expressing himself in dialogue correlates with future change in actual action. It has been shown that how the client articulates his commitments, especially if they evolve during the course of the conversation, predict future behavioral changes in the client (Amrhein, 2004). It has also been shown that the therapist, by acting in accordance with the principles of MI, can increase the chances of her client expressing himself in this way. The therapist's manner can encourage a certain kind of "change talk" in the client, which in turn is a marker for successful change.

---

5   In the following, for the sake of simplicity, I will be referring to the client as "he" and the therapist as "she".

From a behavior analytic perspective it is relatively easy to see how this might work, and such an explanatory model is not dissimilar to the one that MI itself espouses (Christoffer & Dougher, 2009). A therapist acting in accordance with the principles of MI offers an empathetic dialogue in which the client is free to formulate different aspects of his insecurity without judgment; on the contrary, the therapist actively encourages talk of different aspects of the client's ambivalence and the open weighing of options. This increases the likelihood of the client verbalizing different possible strategies and their possible consequences. When the client is thus better able to weigh his options, it is more likely that he will commit to his intentions. Such commitments give the client greater emotional connection with what he wants to achieve (through the formulation of what he considers important); they are also made in the presence of a person who through her dialogue with the client has acquired a certain position—another factor that increases the probability that the client will fulfil what he has undertaken to do.

ACT (acceptance and commitment therapy) is another psychotherapy model that ascribes a high degree of weight to motivational work. ACT is also, more than MI, a therapeutic model born out of behavior analysis. "Commitment" and the therapist's role in helping the client to formulate overarching desirable consequences (values) is one of the pillars of the model. Another aspect of ACT resembles an aspect of MI: that which in ACT goes under the name "creative hopelessness," whereby the therapist identifies through her questions the strategies the client has tried in order to deal with his problem. The open and honest dialogue elucidates the reasonable aspects of the client's efforts to deal with his particular problem. At the same time, the client is encouraged to explore the connection between these strategies and the consequences they have so far had on the basis of his own direct experience. The sought-after "hopelessness" thus refers to current strategies and the experience that they have failed; the "creative" part refers to the possibility that alternative strategies become more accessible to the client through the clarification of the connection between current strategy and undesired consequences. As in MI, the emphasis in ACT is on achieving this not through persuasion or argument on the therapist's part, but through a dialogue that helps the client explore his own experiences and wishes as the basis of continuing action. Both models emphasize the client's own formulated values (what he considers important) as central factors of this motivational work.

Psychoeducation

Most psychotherapeutic models contain elements of education or information, often in the introductory phase of the therapy. Even when this element is not stressed—as is the case, for instance, with classic psychodynamic therapy—it is still there insofar as the therapist provides a certain amount of information on the procedure she will be following and what she expects from her client. In most variants of cognitive behavioral therapy (CBT), psychoeducation is, however, taken to be crucial to the treatment both procedurally and in terms of other phenomenological areas assumed to be of importance to it. In classical cognitive therapy, much is made of the client being informed about what to expect, or of "socializing the client to the model" (Young, Rygh, Weinberger, & Beck, 2014). The same applies to exposure therapy (Neudeck & Einsle, 2012): the client is given a description of the therapeutic process and the reasons behind it. But instruction is given on other things too. Direct information on what anxiety is and the natural place it occupies in human psychology is included in all kinds of CBT for anxiety disorders (Craske & Barlow, 2014). Some form of "affect school" is also common (Mennin, Ellard, Fresco, & Gross 2013; Payne et al., 2014). In dialectical behavior therapy (DBT), much of the group skills training is pure teaching (Linehan, 2015). Two of the therapeutic models that have the best empirical support for treating depression—behavioral activation (Martell, Addis, & Jacobson, 2001) and interpersonal therapy (Weissman, Markowitz, & Klerman, 2000)—include teaching on the mechanisms behind depressive states. In schema therapy, clients are taught about schema (Young, Klosko, & Weishaar, 2003). And even if the teaching component of classic psychodynamic therapy is relatively small, it is not so in its more modern forms. Both treatment for affect phobia (McCullough, Kuhn, Andrews, Kaplan, Wolf, & Lanza Hurley, 2003) and mentalization-based treatment (Bateman & Fonagy, 2006) have a distinct psychoeducative streak. ACT warns against some formal instruction and information on the grounds that it can easily lead to linguistic traps, and stresses more experiential aspects of learning, but this can also be seen as a form of education, albeit via experiential rather than directly instructional elements of the therapy.

Thinking

Thinking is at the heart of cognitive therapy. The focus on how people think and the role it plays in psychological disorders has dominated the field of psychotherapy (and our culture in general) since at least the 1970s. The approach is often encapsulated in a quote from the Greek philosopher Epictetus adopted by the father of cognitive therapy, Aaron Beck: "Men are disturbed not by things, but by the view which they take of them" (Beck, 1976). With this in mind, one of the therapist's most important tasks is to affect how the client "perceives" his situation, his symptoms, or other aspects of his problem. The task is to change the client's way of thinking.

This assumption has been challenged by many researchers and theoreticians in the CBT field in recent years (Longmore & Worrel, 2007); but rather than questioning the idea that human cognition plays a part in psychological problems or that thinking is an important focus for therapy, the object of dispute is how one is to understand the connection between thinking and other behavior, and how the therapeutic strategies are to be designed. One of the therapeutic models that is most vocal in its criticism of the cognitive model is ACT. ACT is based on behavior analysis, which, as we saw in chapter 3, works upon the basic concept that thought, like all other subtle human behavior (feeling, remembering), is to be understood on the same principles as other behavior. Thinking is a behavior that occurs in interaction with the individual's current circumstances, not something that "emerges from within" (Hayes, 1994; 1998). The therapeutic focus is thus on how we interact with our thinking rather than on the content of our cognitions. Both ACT and DBT emphasize training in seeing thoughts for what they are in themselves and on focusing on acceptance and validation (Linehan, 1997). Thinking as an essential human activity of profound significance to human psychology and therefore to therapy is, however, taken for granted.

There are models of cognitive therapy today that share many similarities with ACT, despite the proximity of their theoretical home to Beck's original model. The clearest example of this is metacognitive therapy (Wells, 2005). Here, too, the emphasis is on thinking as an activity—a strategy that needs to be changed—while the importance of the content of thoughts is played down compared to the more original cognitive model. The aim of therapy is for the client to learn to interact (respond) differently in relation to his problematic thoughts rather than modify them. Another example is mindfulness-based cognitive therapy (Segal, Williams, & Teasdale, 2001), which also identifies the main problem as stereotypical interactions with one's thoughts, and focuses therapy on practicing alternative strategies. Similarities can also be seen with certain types of modern psychodynamic therapy, with its emphasis on mentalization (Bateman & Fonagy, 2006).

In all these models, efforts to understand how we think and how this influences psychological problems are central, or at least implicit. All therapies that make use of psychoeducation, for example, make the assumption that the client will remember (in other words, think about) what has been discussed in a later context. Acting in the therapeutic situation in a way that makes this more likely is part of the therapist's job.

Exposure

Exposure is perhaps the psychological therapeutic strategy with the strongest empirical support over a wide array of areas (Barlow, 2002; Neudeck & Wittchen, 2012). It is also an ingredient of treatment models for virtually all types of psychological problems (Barlow, 2014). The basic idea of exposure is that the client is urged to approach the trigger of his anxiety or other negative affect and to refrain from adopting the rigid strategies that this type of situation normally elicits (response prevention). Traditionally, researchers have stressed that change is achieved through the gradual waning of the negative affect. In recent years, other aspects have been brought to the fore, particularly that a greater variability or flexibility in the client's behavioral repertoire (response expansion) in the critical situation increases the chance of change through new learning (Craske, Treanor, Conway, Zbozinek, & Vervliet, 2014).

Exposure can take place in the presence of the therapist or as self-exposure (Craske & Barlow, 2014; Franklin & Foa, 2014). In the first instance, the client and therapist enter or create together the type of situation that is relevant to the client's problem and that is usually associated with problematic avoidance: a real spider for a client with spider phobia, a social interaction for a client with social anxiety disorder, contact with painful memories for a client with post-traumatic stress disorder (PTSD), a situation that typically evokes compulsory behavior for a client with obsessive-compulsive disorder (OCD), and open space for a client with agoraphobia. However, the same principle of exposure to the object of avoidance and practicing of a new strategy can, of course, be applied by the client on his own, often as home assignments in between therapy sessions.

For many types of psychological problems, exposure therapy is described as the "golden standard" and often constitutes the entire therapeutic model for problems like OCD (Franklin & Foa, 2014), specific phobias (Ollendick & Davis, 2013) and PTSD (Foa, Hembree, & Rothbaum, 2007). However, therapeutic models that are described as broader and inclusive of many different interventions, such as ACT (Hayes, Strosahl, & Wilson, 2012), DBT (Neacsiu & Linehan, 2014) and the transdiagnostic model unified protocol (Payne et al., 2014), typically recognize the exposure principle as a critical component.

Emotional Processing

This therapeutic principle very much overlaps the preceding one. In that exposure therapy places the focus on negative affect and the fact that humans easily act dysfunctionally to avoid frightening and painful emotions, there are many points of contact with the models that place particular emphasis on emotional processes and how we learn to deal with them (Greenberg & Pavio, 1997). *Experiential avoidance* (behaving so as to avoid one's own reactions, such as feelings, thoughts, and physical sensations) is an important and problematic psychological process (Hayes, Wilson, Gifford, Follette, & Strosahl, 1996; Chawla & Ostafin, 2007). Acceptance of, and new learning in the presence of, aversive affective states are seen as critical by most evidence-based therapeutic models, variations in theoretical formulations notwithstanding (Bleiberg & Markowitz, 2014; Foa, Huppert, & Cahill, 2006; Hayes, Strosahl & Wilson, 2012; Linehan, 1993; Monson, Resick, & Rizvi, 2014; Payne et al., 2014; Roemer & Orsillo, 2014; Young et al., 2003).

Relationship

The relationship between therapist and client as a crucial catalyst for change has been discussed throughout the history of psychotherapy. At the same time as the research reveals a connection between relational factors and treatment outcomes in a wide range of psychotherapies (Flückiger, Del Re,

Wampold, Symonds, & Horvath, 2011), the discussion has often been polarized, with the so-called therapeutic alliance pitted against a focus on specific techniques (Norcross & Lampert, 2011). From a behavioral standpoint, this is a remarkable polarization. How the therapeutic alliance develops between client and therapist must reasonably depend very much on how the two act toward each other and how they are able to interact. We also know that the collaboration established on goals of treatment affects the therapeutic outcome (Tryon & Winograd, 2011). In other words, it is part of the therapist's job to ensure that an optimal collaboration and alliance are created in the therapeutic dialogue.

In the same way as described under the principle of motivation, different therapeutic models in the evidence-based tradition stress, to different degrees, the relationship as a precondition for treatment and as the very focus of change work. In recent years, closer attention has been paid to the client-therapist interaction in such models as DBT, ACT, and functional analytical psychotherapy (FAP) (Kohlenberg & Tsai, 1991). It is probably no coincidence that all these models are direct applications of basic behavior analytic principles. These points of departure lead inevitably to the following: the only thing to which the therapist has direct access with regard to her client's problems is how they might manifest themselves in their interaction as they meet— everything else is indirect reports by the client (or possibly a third person). The only direct influence the therapist can have is also limited to the occasions on which she actually meets her client. The encounter between client and therapist and the interaction they establish is thus critical. Or to put it another way, we can say that therapy has two scenes (Ramnerö & Törneke, 2008; Törneke, 2010). The first is when the client and therapist meet, and where the actual process of treatment takes place. The second scene is the client's life outside this first scene, where the client wishes for change. The therapist has access only to the first scene for direct intervention. The second scene is something she can only talk about. Just how the therapeutic experience from the first scene can be generalized to the second (the client's life) is thus a key question for all psychotherapy.

Treatment models that do not have this behavioral background also lay emphasis on the "the first scene" interaction and advocate therapeutic interventions targeted accordingly (Safran & Segal, 1990; Safran & Muran, 2000). After reviewing a variety of models in the CBT field, it is also obvious to me that models that do not specifically emphasize the relationship between therapist and client as an area for direct intervention still use this to different degrees (Barlow, 2014). The specific relationship between therapist and client is also the home territory of psychodynamic therapy (Wachtel, 2011).

Proaction

In a sense, proaction can, of course, be said to be the objective of all therapy, in that the client receives help that increases the likelihood that he will adopt new, different behavior in situations that he finds critical and important. A therapeutic model that refines this general truth is behavioral activation as a treatment for depression (Dimidjian, Martell, Herman-Dunn, & Hubley, 2014; Martell et al., 2001), the linchpin of which is the meticulous registration of behavioral strategies. The client is trained to observe what he does in different relevant situations, and the correlations that exist between these concrete actions and his symptoms (principally the client's mood in the treatment of depression). With this analysis as their starting point, the therapist and client search for alternative strategies for the client to try. This approach is a clinical variant of what behavior analysis refers to as *functional analysis* (see chapter 3).

But even if behavioral activation as a model makes a particular unambiguous point of this, the same principle of influencing concrete behavior is an integral part of most evidence-based therapies. In interpersonal therapy, for instance, the therapist uses role-play to practice interpersonal strategies and actively encourages the client to increase and change his social activity. In DBT, concrete skills training is an important ingredient of the treatment (Linehan, 1993; Neacsiu & Linehan, 2014). Cognitive therapy almost always includes a focus on concrete action and experiments in the form of home assignments, even if the theoretical rationale differs from that of behavioral activation (Clark, Ehlers, Hackmann, McManus, Fennell, Grey, et al., 2006; Young et al., 2014). Even a treatment model like mindfulness cognitive therapy (Segal et al., 2001), which is mainly centered on how we relate to our thoughts, contains a distinct element of concrete action, since an important part of the therapy is the client's own actual, concrete exercises. In ACT, the therapist works continuously with identifying and increasing the likelihood that the client will make concrete behavioral changes in line with that to which he ascribes value (Hayes, Strosahl, & Wilson, 2012).

In Search of More Fundamental Principles

I have now given a rough overview of the areas that the evidence-based psychotherapeutic models to varying degrees consider important. To a certain extent, the breakdown into seven areas is of course arbitrary, and the same material could no doubt have been described with a different categorization. That the review covers what is generally considered critical is confirmed by the fact that a relatively new transdiagnostic approach to therapy, referred to as unified protocol, deals with effectively the same areas in its different therapeutic modules (Barlow, 2014; Payne et al., 2014).

However, in the introduction to this chapter, I promised to step from these loosely defined, broadly categorized areas to more fundamental principles of psychological change, and then use these principles as benchmarks for metaphor use in psychotherapy. The reason for my starting from these broad, more general areas is the widespread consensus that exists on them. If it can be convincingly demonstrated that these areas are understandable in terms of more fundamental principles, a number of superficially diverse therapeutic strategies and techniques can be unpacked and their core themes developed. This will give us the more specific focus that we are looking for with regard to metaphor use.

The terms I intend to use for this discussion are *psychological flexibility* and its converse, *psychological inflexibility,* or rigidity, which many scholars have recently identified as being crucial to psychological health in its broad sense and more specifically to different kinds of psychopathology (Bond, Hayes, Baer, Carpenter, Guenole, et al., 2011; Bryan, Ray-Sannerud, & Heron, 2015; Gloster, Klotsche, Chaker, Hummel, & Hoyer, 2011; Kashdan & Rottenberg, 2010; Levin, Luoma, Vilardaga, Lillis, Nobles, et al., 2015; Levin, MacLane, Daflos, Seeley, Hayes, et al., 2014). These terms are also central to the understanding of therapeutic strategies in ACT (Ciarrochi, Bilich, & Godsel, 2010; Hayes, Strosahl, & Wilson, 2012). A corresponding concept used in the field of new learning through exposure is *variability* (Craske et al., 2014.), which refers to the context that is to be established in the therapeutic situation (which is to be varied) in order to achieve flexibility.

One vital aspect of psychological flexibility/inflexibility is our ability to relate to our own emotions, thoughts, and responses in general (Bond et al., 2011; Levin et al., 2014), and our ending up in vicious circles in this respect is seen as a core part of psychological problems. We are overcontrolled by our own responses, which often prompts us to make unproductive attempts to rid ourselves of spontaneously aroused emotions, thoughts, memories, and physical reactions. This "experiential avoidance" (Chawla & Ostafin, 2007; Hayes et al., 1996) often impedes other more effective and meaningful behavioral strategies.

From this point of view, increasing psychological flexibility is the very essence of psychological therapy and thus the principle that should also guide the use of metaphors in psychotherapy.

RFT and Psychological Flexibility

From the perspective of RFT, psychological flexibility is a result of a special way of interacting with your own responding (Törneke, Luciano, Barnes-Holmes, & Bond, 2016). Let me start by giving a brief précis of the theoretical background to this before turning to the practical clinical principles that ensue therefrom and that can serve as a way in for metaphor use.

That we learn from the early days of language acquisition to relate phenomena on the basis of arbitrary contextual cues (see chapter 4) dramatically increases our behavioral flexibility. Things are no longer what they are merely in terms of their physical characteristics, but also in terms of how we have learned to relate them to other phenomena. And this we do via a learned "game" in which different contextual cues (largely words but also, for example, gestures) govern how we relate. This also means that phenomena that we may observe in ourselves (emotions, thoughts, memories, physical sensations) can have a variety of functions for us depending on how we have learned to relate them to other things. These inherently subtle or private events can thus become dangerous, wonderful, repulsive, and meaningful regardless of what they are "in themselves." They are given a "meaning" and can thus have a profound and lasting influence on all our other behavior. This is essentially useful as we can therefore shape the way in which we continue to behave (Luciano et al., 2009.) We can think, "That is dangerous" about something of which we have no experience and adopt a response of avoidance accordingly.

Or we can think, "If I do that, it'll pay off in the long run," and act in a way that in the short-term only causes discomfort, but that allows us to attain something we might never have otherwise attained. We can "rise above immediate gratification" and act in the interest of long-term consequences. We set up goals and then act in accordance with what are our own verbal formulations (Ramnerö & Törneke, 2015). In behavior analysis, this ability is usually referred to as "rule-governed behavior" and denotes the same phenomenon that would be described more generally in psychology as our ability to follow instructions.

In essence, this ability enhances human flexibility with regard to interaction with both the social and the material environment. But it has a flipside, a side effect if you like, in the form of the psychological inflexibility referred to above. The very fact that our rule following is largely of social origin makes us vulnerable. We have been shaped not only by our direct experience but also by how we have learned to relate the one to the other. If I have learned to relate particular emotions to threat, particular memories to "what ruined my life," or particular responses as in opposition to what constitutes "a good life," it can have a profound impact on the way I behave. Acting on many of these "self-rules" can be the result of practice over long periods of time, and I behave accordingly without being cognizant of the way certain rules influence my behavior.

This type of inflexibility is part of normal human psychology; however, when it generalizes, we approach that which we are accustomed to calling psychopathology (Törneke, Luciano, & Valdivia-Salas, 2008). Our own reactions and our ability to interact with them are thus a boon but also a risk, especially if we receive inadequate training in how to approach them effectively. However, such training is part of early language acquisition. At the same time as we learn the ability to follow instructions and gradually develop self-rules, we learn to interact with our own emotions, thoughts, memories, and the rules created out of these phenomena (Luciano et al., 2009). A critical skill in this process is that which I described above under the heading deictic framing (see chapter 4). This means that we learn to relate to that which we can observe in ourselves from the perspective of "I-here-now," the perspective from which, once we have learned it, we always interact with everything we encounter (McHugh & Stewart, 2012). From this vantage point, we are able to observe and relate not only to the external environment but also to our own responding, such as emotions, memories, and physical sensations. We learn to relate to our own reactions and the concomitant self-rules as being part of us (hierarchical framing), at the same time as we can also distinguish ourselves from them ("I am here and notice that as part of me"—deictic and hierarchical framing) and retain the ability to choose what to do (Luciano, Ruiz, Vizcaino-Torres, Sánches-Martin, Martinez, et al., 2011). One could say that we learn to establish an observational distance from our reactions. The point is that we are not just to act immediately to everything that emerges within ourselves, but also to interact with these automatically triggered responses in such a way that benefits our life. There is today broad consensus that learning to practice this repertoire is an important psychotherapeutic process (Bernstein, Hadash, Lichtash, Tanay, Shepherd, et al., 2015). What RFT brings to this knowledge is operationalized concepts and closer links to basic research. RFT allows us to characterize this repertoire as framing our own responses as participating in a frame of hierarchy with the deictic self (Törneke et al., 2016). *It is this skill that is at the core of psychological flexibility, and therefore it is the central task of the therapist to train her client in this repertoire* (Foody, Barnes-Holmes, Barnes-Holmes, & Luciano, 2013; Foody, Barnes-Holmes, Barnes-Holmes, Rai, & Luciano, 2015; Luciano et al., 2011).

Training in Psychological Flexibility

The following three principles are proffered as being essential strategies for the therapist wishing to help her client improve his psychological flexibility, as described in the previous section. They are not necessarily to be applied in any particular order, but are to be considered more as parallel features of the therapeutic process; and while they partially overlap, rather than being distinct, they are nevertheless presented separately so that they can be used to guide clinical work, including the use of metaphors.

- Help the client discern the relationship between what he does and the problematic consequences he experiences.

- Help the client discern his own thoughts, emotions, and physical sensations by establishing an observational distance from them as they emerge.

- Help the client use this skill to clarify what is important in his life and what would be concrete steps in that direction.

Let me now give a brief account of each of these principles and show how they underpin the different broader areas that I have described in this chapter. How metaphors can be used as a key component of doing precisely this will be the theme of the remainder of this book.

Help the client discern the relationship between what he does and the problematic consequences he experiences

If the key aspect of psychological flexibility is how you interact with your own behavior, then recognizing your own behavior and how it links to other events is crucial. To quote a now antiquated assertion by Skinner: "A person who has been 'made aware of himself' by the questions he has been asked is in a better position to predict and control his own behavior" (Skinner, 1974, p. 35). To ask questions to this effect is a starting point of therapy and a base upon which the two following principles build.

In clinical behavior analysis this therapeutic strategy is usually referred to as a functional analysis or an ABC (antecedent-behavior-consequence) analysis (Ramnerö & Törneke, 2008). By going through repeated examples of situations the client finds distressing or troubling, the therapist and client together identify antecedent factors (A) to the client's behavior (B) and the resulting consequences (C) in order to help the client eventually develop alternative strategies. As things progress, this therapeutic approach necessarily constitutes work with motivation and psychoeducation: motivation, since a clear experience of the consequences of our behavior affects our inclination to do the one thing or the other; psychoeducation, since a careful review of these links boosts the client's faculty for learning with regard to the problems with which he is wrestling, and gives the therapist a variety of means by which she may illustrate for the client how central processes operate.

This approach will also very probably constitute work with thinking, exposure, and emotional processing. Modes of thinking that are central to the client and different kinds of emotional states often both comprise important components of what in a functional analysis are called antecedents; in other words, it is in the presence of certain thoughts and feelings that current problematic behavioral strategies occur. The therapist thus directs attention to these phenomena in these analyses and examines her client's strategies. Since problematic strategies commonly comprise attempts to avoid automatically triggered emotional reactions, the very focus that a functional analysis trains on these phenomena can serve as an exposure to them, and an emotional processing of them.

A functional analysis can also be made of the alternative strategies with which the client experiments as a part of therapeutic work. Proaction is thus encouraged, either explicitly or implicitly.

The client-therapist relationship is also a possible focus for this approach. Together with her client, the therapist seeks problematic strategies, which may then be made the focus of functional analysis if and when they appear in the therapeutic interaction. If the client, for example, falls silent or becomes belligerent, dismissive, or seductive in a way that can be seen as illustrative of his problem, it can be made the object of functional analysis. What was the antecedent to his behavior here and now (A)? Something the therapist said or did? What, exactly, did the client do (B)? What followed (C)?

Ideally, making a functional analysis like this with the client also leads us into the second fundamental principle.

Help the client discern his own thoughts, emotions, and physical sensations by establishing an observational distance from them as they emerge

Psychological inflexibility, as understood by RFT, constitutes our tendency to interact with our own reactions without distinguishing them from ourselves as acting beings. In a sense this is not strange; after all, our own reactions are an aspect of ourselves. This way of interacting with ourselves is not problematic when it refers to individual events; the problems arise when it is generalized to multiple or single critical spheres of our lives, at which point the behavioral pattern can obstruct the application of other, more effective strategies.

Developing the ability to establish an observational distance from our own reactions in situations when these reactions (what we feel, think, sense, and

remember) risk misguiding us is absolutely essential to all work with psychological change and is the core of psychological flexibility training.

Of the more loosely defined areas that I described at the start of this
chapter, there are some more explicitly based on this therapeutic strategy.
Working with the client's thinking is one. What we think, the meaning we
ascribe to an event, and what we infer from something is part of our own reaction and thus the phenomenon that needs discerning. It is to be heeded and
distinguished as part of me, and yet not as identical to me as an acting being.
I am to practice my ability to notice my own responding from the perspective
that I call "I" and thus establish an observational distance. I can think in a
certain way and then choose what to do next. The same thing applies to what
is called emotional processing. I observe what I feel and sense and then choose
how I am to act; this rather than merely reacting more or less automatically to
whatever is occurring. Since some of these spontaneous emotional reactions
are aversive and have been the object of avoidance, this therapeutic strategy
also constitutes exposure.

What is specifically practiced in this work has already had its foundations
laid in the functional analysis that I described above. In functional analysis, as
we have seen, there is an element of observation, of noticing that "this is something I think/feel/remember." Another demonstration of the overlap of the
principles for training in psychological flexibility is the attitude adopted when
dealing with the content of spontaneously aroused thoughts. How the client
perceives an event is analytically important for understanding, but the focus is
not on whether his spontaneously aroused thought or reaction is correct or
not. It is directed at what the client does in this situation, given that he thinks
and feels in just the way he thinks and feels, and at what the consequences of
this are (A—B—C!).

Help the client use this skill to clarify what is important in his life and what would be concrete steps in that direction

When describing the problems that can arise in the interaction we have
with our thoughts and feelings, it is easy to overlook the fact that our ability to
interact with our own responses is essentially an asset and a vital tool for

negotiating our external milieu. In this third therapeutic principle, workability is in focus. The ability to establish an observational distance from our own reactions can be used to direct our actions toward that which is important to us (Gil-Luciano, Ruiz, Valdivia-Salas, & Suárez-Falcón, 2016). It is the decisive advantage gained from being able to follow instructions or rules: we can rise above immediate gratification and act in the interests of valued ends, of whatever we believe to be important in the longer term. For many clients, this presents itself more or less automatically when they have learned a new approach to their responses that once led to problematic behavioral strategies. Others need more active interventions from the therapist before they can use their own feelings and thoughts to direct their actions to things they value.

This therapeutic principle places the focus on motivation. If you no longer let yourself be inhibited or controlled by everything that is automatically aroused in you and, instead, notice all this and choose your direction for yourself, what then is important? If what were once controlling reactions no longer have you in their grasp, where will you go? What active steps can you now take that are faithful to what you judge to be important, to what you value? Raised here are issues of proaction.

This also leads to exposure. If the client takes new steps, it is likely that previously avoided phenomena will present themselves. Memories, thoughts, feelings, and physical sensations that have had an obstructive function are triggered once more, and the therapeutic work resorts to the preceding principle, so that the client must once again encounter and notice his own reactions. This reconnects with functional analysis and the exploration of effective action given the reactions that arise. If the client then does new things, he will encounter new consequences, thus creating opportunities for new learning.

Conclusion—and a Warning

One conclusion that can be drawn from the research on metaphor use in psychotherapy is that it is not enough to focus merely on metaphor use per se; we need also to identify events of particular clinical interest before seeing how metaphors can be used in precisely these sequences. In this chapter I have tried to formulate such events—firstly by broadly describing areas of clinical intervention on which there is general consensus about their significance, then by presenting three basic therapeutic strategies on which these areas depend:

a) help the client discern the relationship between what he does and the problematic consequences he experiences; b) help the client discern his own thoughts, emotions, and physical sensations by establishing an observational distance from them as they emerge; and c) help the client use this skill to clarify what is important in his life and what would be concrete steps in that direction.

These three strategies thus guide the clinician as to when and how metaphors can be used in psychotherapy. Hopefully, this will also create points of contact between clinical work and basic research, since these three principles are closely linked to phenomena that can be recreated under controlled laboratory settings.

In this chapter, the principles have been painted in broad strokes without clinical examples. Such examples and a more practical account of how these principles can guide metaphor use in psychotherapeutic practice make up the remainder of this book.

Let me close this chapter, however, with a warning. The following clinical discussions and examples are wholly dominated by metaphor use. This does not mean that a more literal use of language is in any way less important in psychotherapy. As I pointed out earlier, I am not presenting a kind of "metaphor therapy." Even if metaphors have a much more critical function in human language than once thought, humans have also developed a more abstract "literal" language, which has both meaning and function. That little interest is paid to it in the following chapters is not to imply that it is of less importance, only that the focus of this book lies elsewhere.

CHAPTER 8

Creating Metaphors for Functional Analysis

Most metaphors in a normal dialogue are spontaneous and not contrived by the speaker, not the product of "cunning invention." Most metaphors are dead or frozen, and were integrated into common parlance in the mists of etymological history, as is well demonstrated by much contemporary research (see chapters 1 and 2). Most texts describing metaphor use in psychotherapy, however, lay the focus on metaphors of the "cunning" kind, which is to say those that the user invents in advance in order to illustrate something that the therapeutic model defines as important (see, for example, Barker, 1985; Blenkiron, 2010; Stoddard & Afari, 2014; Stott et al., 2010). This is natural since one may expect therapeutic models to contain elements that they deem essential for adoption by the client. At the same time, this approach is in danger of overlooking the more subtle functions of metaphors, not least when they are used spontaneously, perhaps even unwittingly. There are also models of metaphor use in psychotherapy that run with this second premise, most explicitly so in books lying outside the evidence-based tradition (Kopp, 1995; Sullivan & Rees, 2008). As explained in this book's theoretical section, there are many reasons to take note of this "unintentional" kind of metaphor use, and I will be returning to this matter in a later chapter. Let me begin, however, with the "intentional" coining of a metaphor, where the therapist creates a metaphor with a particular purpose in mind. This I want to do partly because I believe that metaphors are to be used for specific ends (as explained in the previous chapter) and partly because it is a natural way to illustrate how metaphors can operate in psychotherapeutic contexts.

Source and Target of Clinical Metaphors

The metaphor's target is the phenomenological area that the therapist wishes to draw attention to or influence, and its source is the phenomenological area she uses for this purpose. To put this in RFT terms, we could say that the therapist relates two relational networks: the target and the source (see chapter 4). Let me give a simple clinical example.

Barry[6], a retired truck driver, suffers from chronic pain and depression. He has explained to his therapist that he refrains from doing things that he once did and that he wants to get back to again. The same theme reemerges.

> *Therapist:*   How did it go with calling your brother? Did you speak to him?
>
> *Barry:*   No, I didn't get around to it. I'll do it another time. I was in so much pain last week that I just couldn't be bothered.
>
> *Therapist:*   Okay. So you've simply parked. (Figure 8.1)

In this example, the therapist decides to make Barry's behavior—his refraining from calling his brother—the metaphor's target; its source is "to park." Let us use this simple example to spotlight some key aspects of metaphor use in change work.

Two networks are related. The metaphor's target (Barry not calling his brother) is not a random choice, but is yet another instance of a recurrent behavior pattern that Barry has reproduced on many previous occasions: blaming his failure to perform a desired act on pain and despondency. The therapist chooses this target for the metaphor, having judged that this strategy is a relevant aspect of Barry's problem. This is the first important principle of metaphor creation in change work: *the metaphor's target must be a phenomenon that has an important function for the individual client.* The choice of target for a metaphor must therefore be based on a functional assessment on the part of the therapist (Foody, Barnes-Holmes, Barnes-Holmes, Törneke, Luciano, et al., 2014). The choice of source is also, of course, clinically relevant, and obeys its own principle: *the metaphor's source must correspond to essential features of its*

---

6   All names and cases in this book are fictional but hopefully recognisable as authentic to practising therapists.

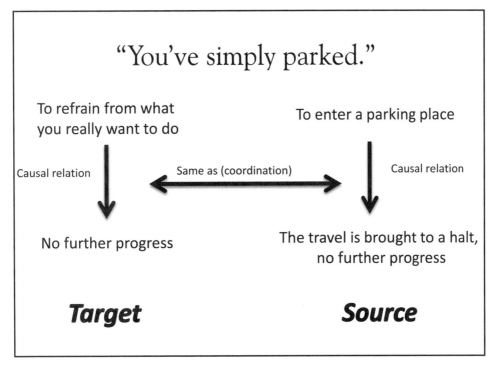

"You've simply parked."

To refrain from what you really want to do

To enter a parking place

Causal relation

Same as (coordination)

Causal relation

No further progress

The travel is brought to a halt, no further progress

Target

Source

Figure 8.1

target. Put simply: the source must be such that the client recognizes his experience in the metaphor. In Barry's case, it is vital that when he hears the therapist say, "Okay. So you've simply parked," he recognizes that this is an apposite description of what he does when, for instance, refraining from calling his brother. To find a source like this naturally takes fair knowledge of the client, and presumably increases the likelihood that the client will feel understood. The source "park" for the target "to not do something you want to" is readily identifiable, assuming that the client has a car and knows what it is like to park it. However, if the client does not drive and never has, the metaphor might then be a poorly chosen one. Barry's therapist, however, knows that he worked as a truck driver and thus guesses that the metaphor will resonate with him, something that she confirms only when Barry interacts with what she has just said. It does not matter if the therapist deems her metaphor to be "correct" if it is of no apparent benefit to the therapeutic work.

There is another property of the source that is required for the metaphor to be effective or to have at least some impact on the hearer. This is the third principle of metaphor creation: *the metaphor's source must contain a property or function that is more salient there than it is in the metaphor's target.* It is the important function that the therapist intends to highlight or emphasize by using the metaphor. It is the very point of the metaphor—its "bite," so to speak. In Barry's case, the concept of "parking" must bring to greater clarity an aspect of his behavior that is less obvious in the expression "refraining from calling his brother." As described earlier when discussing metaphors more generally, this property often exists in the metaphor's target but not explicitly so (see chapter 4). The very point of using a metaphor is that this property also becomes evident in its target when it is heard. Compare with Tomas Tranströmer's poetic metaphor "Waking up is a parachute jump from the dream." The simple fact that the listener recognizes something in her experience of waking up when reading the metaphor is the point. The metaphor's source (a parachute jump) has properties that to some degree, but less explicitly, exist in its target (the experience of waking up). The metaphor's bite is its ability to elucidate or emphasize this property of the target.

So what is it that the therapist wants Barry to take note of in his behavior of "refraining from calling his brother"? Possibly the following consequences: If you are out driving and then park somewhere, you will make no further progress; you can stop for a while and drive off again, of course, but the act of parking per se is the antithesis of driving to wherever you wish to go—at least if you park often, and especially if you park as soon as you enter a road that leads to some important destination. However, it is only if three fundamentals coincide that this metaphor will say anything of meaning to Barry: Firstly, his refraining behavior must be part of his problem; secondly, the use of the word "park" must resonate with him and his experience of refraining; and thirdly, the word "park" must also make clear to Barry something in his behavior that he would benefit from discerning (see figure 8.2).

Shifting Source and Target

If a metaphor, such as "to park," is effective, it can be used as a source for additional metaphorical targets. Say that the metaphor is initially established in a conversation, as above, on concrete actions, like refraining to call a brother. At

---

Three principles of metaphor creation in clinical work

- *The metaphor's target must be a phenomenon that has an important function for the individual client.*

- *The metaphor's source must correspond to essential features of its target.*

- *The metaphor's source must contain a property or function that is more salient there than it is in the metaphor's target.*

Figure 8.2

a later stage, Barry might talk about failing to do something he planned to do in another, hitherto unmentioned part of his life. The therapist can then use the same source to ask, "Are you parking here too, or is it something else?" Using the same source for different targets can help with encapsulation and focus and can be particularly important to functional analysis and self-observation training (see below).

A certain source can, of course, be insufficient for talking about a certain process. If so, the therapist might have to resort to another source to talk about the same metaphorical target. Let's say that Barry describes a new aspect of his behavior:

Barry: I just don't get around to it. But it's not like I've just parked and am just sitting there. It sounds as if I'm able to sit back and take a rest, but I really don't do that. It's such a struggle.

Therapist: It's something you struggle with, something you try to achieve?

Barry: Yes, I don't know what I'd say to him if I ever did get
              hold of him. I've thought through so many options but
              I can't find anything. Nothing seems suitable. I try to
              think of something but whatever I come up with just
              feels so vacuous. I can't think of anything sensible.

Therapist: It's as if you're looking for your keys but can't find them.

Here, the dialogue is still about Barry refraining from calling his brother
(the metaphor's target), but with a new source, introduced in an attempt to
shed new light on Barry's experience and behavior. "Looking for your keys but
can't find them" could be a way of addressing the role that ruminating has in
his habit of "parking." If Barry can relate to this, this metaphorical source can
also be used in conversations about targets other than calling his brother—
such as with the question, "What I said about looking for keys you can't find,
do you recognize that from other situations in which you've felt troubled?" Or
maybe in a later conversation, perhaps about Barry's attitude to his pain, the
therapist can use this metaphorical source to talk about some other observation she has made:

Barry: This is what's constantly on my mind and that just goes
              round and round in my head. What's wrong with me?
              There must be something, given the pain I have. But you
              know they find nothing, or at least not much. What
              causes this pain?

Therapist: This question comes up for you a lot, if I'm not
              mistaken.

Barry: All the time!

Therapist: I wonder. When you try to answer these questions
              without finding an answer, are you just parking and
              looking in vain for your keys all over again?

Using the same source for different targets can help to summarize and tie
together different areas of the client's problem. Using different sources for the
same target can help to deepen and nuance the dialogue (Tay, 2013).

Metaphors for Functional Analysis

Chapter 7 described three fundamental strategies for therapeutic conversations. Let us now see how metaphors can be used in their practical application. Although the strategies overlap each other, I shall try to stress the aspects that are typical to each one. We begin with functional analysis.

The aim of this strategy is to help the client understand the connections between the strategies he currently uses and the difficulties he experiences. Put simply: What do you do; under what circumstances do you do it; what consequences does it have and what are you trying to achieve? This is not primarily an intellectual process but very much a matter of making experiential contact with how these phenomena go together. The consequences of our actions have a powerful influence on our continuing actions. At the same time, our ability to follow rules has a number of side effects in the form of rigid behavioral strategies that make us insensitive to some consequences. As described in chapter 7, we easily act on the basis of rules and self-instructions that draw us into vicious circles in the form, say, of experiential avoidance. If we carefully observe what we do—how we interact with our own emotions, thoughts, and physical sensations, and the consequences of that interaction—we would be better able to effect change. Metaphors can fulfill a pivotal function in this respect.

Metaphors for the Link Between Behavior and Consequence

The case of Barry can be slotted in under this heading. A functional analysis seeks a description of the sequence: Antecedent circumstances (A), the ensuing Behavior (B), and the Consequences that result (C). When the therapist uses the word "park," she is placing the focus on what Barry does (on B) in order to make the consequence (C) clearer to Barry and hopefully affect his behavior in similar future situations. To talk in this way of what someone does in typical problem situations and help the client to identify the consequences becomes what in ACT is refered to as "creative hopelessness" (see chapter 7).

Let me give an example of a metaphor that can be used with precisely this focus. Like many of the metaphors used in ACT (Hayes, Strosahl, & Wilson,

2012; Stoddard & Afari, 2014), this is one that is assumed to be of relatively general utility since it is constructed to shed light on a common psychological phenomenon: the fact that we easily go on doing something even though we, in a sense, know it is not working for what we want.

Let us assume that the therapist is in dialogue with Catherine, a museum worker, who describes herself as stressed, anxious, and tired, and repeatedly complains of not getting done the things she feels she needs to do. She claims to enjoy her job, but feels that her workload just gets heavier and heavier. However, she is appreciated by her colleagues and praised for "having everything under control so that it gets done." It has been like this for many years.

Catherine: That's me all over. I take responsibility, always have.

Therapist: Okay. And it leads to many good things, if I understand you correctly?

Catherine: Well, in a way—though not any more at work. I'm totally exhausted. It's not working. I do my best but I can't take it any more, I can see that.

Therapist: When you do your best, what is it you do?

Catherine: I guess it's keeping tabs on things so that everything gets seen to properly. And every*one*, for that matter. People have gotten used to me sorting things out. It's sometimes as if they don't care. I mean, they're good colleagues, but many of them just let things go too easily.

Therapist: And you're the one who makes sure things get done?

Catherine: Yes, someone has to.

Therapist: And how does that work out?

Catherine: It's not actually working out for me at all any more. I find it exhausting.

Therapist: It makes me think of what it can be like trying to shift a heavy rock with an iron bar. Have you ever done that?

Catherine: Yes, sure. My husband and I have kind of inverted gender roles when it comes to yard work. He's totally uninterested so I'm the one who does that stuff at home. Mostly, at least.

Therapist: Okay. Imagine that you've come across a huge rock when out doing the yard work. You try with all your might but you can't shift it. You try different angles. You try sticking the lever as far as you can under it. You try using your body weight to increase the force by leaning on the end of the lever. Nothing. You think, *This must be possible*, and try again. Deeper with the bar, a new angle. No good. You maybe think, *I need another lever, a better lever, a golden lever*, but none of it helps. The rock just sits there, heavy and unmovable. And I wonder, isn't this a bit what it's like at work? You try to get everything done, to take responsibility for sorting everything out—in a variety of ways, as you've described. Every day, the same struggle. And I wonder: do you ever shift that rock?

Note that the therapist describes the metaphor's source (moving a rock in the garden) relatively vividly, with different concrete scenarios. The more the source is embedded in the client's own experience, the better. The therapist then returns the dialogue to what she intends as the metaphor's target: the client's manner at work. Just as in the case with the narrower metaphor "to park," three things are needed for this metaphor to be of use to Catherine.

1. The metaphor's target (Catherine's strategy of taking responsibility, of sorting everything out) must be functionally important—in other words, part of Catherine's problem.

2. The metaphor's source must correspond to central parts of its target. In this case, Catherine must recognize her strategy at work in the description of what it is like to try to shift a heavy rock.

3. The metaphor's source must embody a property or function that is more salient there than it is in its target. The fact of becoming tired and worn out in the face of fruitless labor is more tangible in the

description of shifting the stone than it has been for Catherine in what she tries at work. But the very point of employing the metaphor is to shed light on this aspect of Catherine's way of acting at her job and thus, hopefully, affect her behavior (see fig. 8.3).

Another metaphor that could be used for the same purpose would be to say to Catherine, "It's as if you keep running and running. The question is: Do you ever reach your destination?"

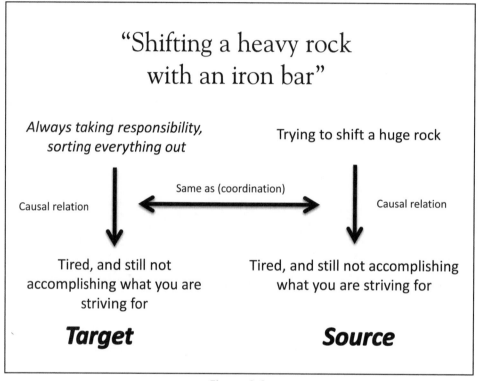

Figure 8.3

Another metaphor, used in ACT, to similarly illustrate a futile behavioral strategy and its consequences is "digging in a hole" (Hayes, Strosahl, & Wilson, 2012). This metaphor can be presented like this:

> *Therapist:*   Let's assume that, for some strange reason, you've been blindfolded and led into a field and told to walk around. You're given a bag of tools to carry that you can use if

you get into difficulties. Now, what you don't know, and can't see, is that in this field there are a number of widely spaced, fairly deep holes. So sooner or later you fall into one. You try to climb out but you can't. You remember the bag and check inside it. What you find is a shovel. So you dutifully start digging, naturally, as you've been given a shovel and been told it's useful. You try to dig a kind of staircase. But the soil is loose and the steps crumble underfoot. You get desperate and start digging and digging, but you risk just making the hole bigger—and deeper.

Being confronted with the fact that one's own strategies are part of one's problems can be painful. So it is important that in doing this, the therapist also points out the reasonable side of the client's behavior. The strategy of "doing what you've learned to do and trying to do it better" is in many ways reasonable and something we all apply to many areas of our lives. We obey different rules and instructions, we have been "given a tool bag," we have good reason to want to "shift the rock," and when we think we need to hurry we "run." There is nothing unusual about that. The catch is, of course, that we can end up exerting ourselves in vain and becoming trapped in a vicious circle, blind to the link between B and C—what we do, and what we get.

The very correlation between behavior and consequence (what we do and what we get as a result of what we have done) lies at the heart of the functional analysis. Realizing that I do things that just exacerbate my problem can be painful, sometimes very much so, yet this is where the potential for change lies. If what I do is irrelevant, if my only problem is that I suffer from something over which I have no control, how will I then be able to effect change? The client's ability to change his behavior with the assistance that the therapy hopefully provides is the self-evident point of departure for all psychotherapy. Therefore, efforts to help the client make the connection between his own behavior and its consequences are wholly decisive. However, there is in one sense a step preceding this: discerning what one does. It is the job of the therapist to use what she suspects to be the locus of the connections to direct the client's attention in the right direction. At the same time, especially early on in the therapy, there can be reason not to be too hasty in placing so much focus on the B-C connection and to merely note what the client does. This might be because the therapist is not yet clear in her mind about where the correlations are and has to feel her way forward, or because it is painful to the client and if the therapist pounces too swiftly it can harm the cooperation. Such considerations affect the way metaphors are used in this clinical situation. In the case of both the rock and the hole, the focus is on the futility of the strategy. Let us return to Barry and his "parking" behavior to see how this can be used to fix attention solely on his behavior and not on its effectiveness—or lack thereof.

Therapist:	Okay, so you've simply parked.
Barry:	You could say that, yes. It's all I can do. I have to. Otherwise I just get nowhere.
Therapist:	*(suspecting that she has brought up the B-C association too early)* Yes, it's as if you need to take a break. This parking thing—is it something you'd say you do a lot? I mean with things other than calling your brother?

The therapist notes that the metaphor seems to have resonated as a description of what Barry does even if the connection with its negative consequences is kept out of the equation. And she tries to apply the metaphor's source to other situations on the basis of her analysis that this strategy has to be explored more closely. If the conditions for an effective metaphor are fulfilled (1. This is part of Barry's problem; 2. Barry recognizes his behavior; 3. The word "park" clarifies some important aspect of this behavioral strategy), the therapist's question can help Barry to recognize what he does. If Barry answers her question by providing more examples of occasions when he "parks," the therapist will be able to return to the connection the strategy has with its potentially deleterious consequences.

Metaphors for the link between antecedents and behavior

There is also reason to look at the other link of the functional sequence of Antecedent-Behavior-Consequence (ABC), namely the link between the preceding circumstances to what we do, and our behavior (A and B). Normally the focus of functional analysis for nonhuman animals is exclusively on the extraneous circumstances that precede and evoke a certain behavior. This is, naturally, also important for humans. Catherine's efforts, for example, are made under certain external circumstances at her workplace. But as we saw in chapter 7, our faculty for relational framing can often cause our own responses or reactions to have a highly complex effect on the rest of our behavior. This is an important part of the circumstances that affect our problematic behavioral strategies and is something of which we need to be attentive in our attempts, in Skinner's words, to "be aware of ourselves to predict and control our behavior."

I have already mentioned that experiential avoidance (the way we try to eliminate, reduce, or control our own thoughts, feelings, and physical sensations) is often a key strategy in psychological problems (Chawla & Ostafin 2007; Hayes et al., 1996; Kashdan, Barrios, Forsyth, & Steger, 2006). It is precisely this kind of strategy in which we easily become trapped despite its ineffectiveness in giving us what we seek. Let us return to Barry. As we saw in the earlier dialogue, the therapist focused on what Barry did ("park") and the link between that and the following consequences. Here is another dialogue in which the therapist turns her attention to the circumstances preceding his behavior that Barry describes as feelings of despondency. Again she uses a metaphor, one intended to help Barry identify the dilemma of experiential avoidance—and that also hints at an alternative.

> *Therapist:* It's common these days for people to compare humans and how we work with computers. Sure it can be a bit over the top, but there is one thing I think can be compared: pop-ups. You know, those little messages that suddenly appear on the screen and that either give information or tell you to do things. Know what I mean?
>
> *Barry:* Yeah, I know what a pop-up is. But what are you...?
>
> *Therapist:* What I'm getting at is that we all get pop-ups, all the time. Thoughts pop up—memories, feelings, and so on. Even when we're sitting here. I imagine you just had one: *What is she getting at?*
>
> *Barry:* Okay, I get it. Yeah, that happens all the time.

Therapist: Most pop-ups are pretty mundane. We're reminded of things we have to do, like pick up a carton of milk on the way home from work. But some are painful, like the one you describe as you being despondent. The one that popped up when you first had the idea of calling your brother, for example. What does that pop-up contain?

Barry: It's the pain and a heavy feeling. There's like no point. I don't know what to say to him. And what will he say to me?

Therapist: So one thing in this pop-up is a question—or rather, two questions. *What will I say? What's he going to say?* And then the pain and that heavy feeling.

Barry: Yes, that's where I get stuck.

Therapist: That's when you park.

Barry: Exactly.

Therapist: I'm thinking this is where humans and computers differ. You know, computers have applications that allow you to shut off pop-ups. Block them.

Barry: That'd be something—if I could shut off all the questions and heavy feelings. I just haven't figured out how to. Got any techniques for doing that?

Therapist: I'm afraid not. It's just how we are. But here's one important point: What if the pop-ups aren't actually the problem? They can ask difficult questions and be painful, but that's not the critical issue. The problem is not that they pop up, it's when we go in and start clicking on them. They ask questions and we go in and try to answer them. They remind us of painful memories or thoughts and we try to get rid of them. But all that happens is that we get stuck. What if you don't have to shut them off? If you can just leave them be? You can't stop them popping up but you don't have to click on them.

Barry: And do what?

Therapist: Well, maybe don't point the mouse at the pop-up, and
            move the cursor over to the main screen instead. Be
            open to other things that are there. Don't try to get rid of
            them, but don't go clicking on them either. Make room
            for the important things, the things in the main window.

This last comment of the therapist's introduces a new theme, namely what Barry could do instead of what he is accustomed to doing in these situations. We will return to this theme when illustrating how to work with the third therapeutic strategy I have proposed: clarifying what is important in one's life and taking steps in that direction. Here, however, I wish to concentrate on the metaphor that is intended to shed light on the connection between Barry's responses (feelings and thoughts) and what he does, and the fact that he has a choice. And again, if this metaphor is to be useful:

1. The metaphor's target (Barry's experience of despondency and what he does in its presence) must be functionally important—in other words, part of Barry's problem.

2. The metaphor's source must correspond to central parts of its target. In this case, Barry must recognize his experience in the description of the interaction with pop-ups on a computer screen.

3. The metaphor's source must embody a property or function that is more salient there than it is in its target. The fact that we can choose how to respond to some seemingly important thing that pops up to grab our attention is more tangible in the description of the interaction with the computer than it has been for Barry with regard to his way of behaving in the presence of his despondency and difficult questions. But the very point of employing the metaphor is to shed light on this and thus, hopefully, affect Barry's behavior.

Another metaphor designed to illustrate the same relationship between personal responses in the form of emotions, thoughts, and physical sensations and the ensuing behavior is that of "road signs." Let us return to Catherine and her situation at work.

Therapist: Can we take a closer look at a situation when things get really tough for you? You just said that yesterday was hell. Was it a typical example?

Catherine: Yes, it was. It was awful. And if it goes on like that I don't know how I'll be able to carry on.

Therapist: When did it start?

Catherine: Just after the morning coffee break. I got several urgent emails and then Petra came by with material that had to be looked at before the meeting we're having on Friday. It all just kind of overflowed.

Therapist: Was that an example of their unreasonable expectations that you'll take care of it?

Catherine: In a way, but not really. I mean, she did say it could wait until next week, but that's easy to say. By then there'll be even more stuff!

Therapist: What pops up in that situation? (The therapist uses the present tense to help Catherine capture spontaneous responses.)

Catherine: What do you mean, 'pops up'?

Therapist: What do you feel, what goes through your head?

Catherine: I get stressed, hot, and I can feel my heart pounding. I won't have time.

Therapist: Have time…to get things done?

Catherine: Exactly. No chance. I can often stay late, but yesterday I couldn't.

Therapist: So what do you do, in that situation?

Catherine: There's not much I can do. Just plug away at it as hard as I can. Miss lunch, rush things…Hopeless!

Therapist: I'm thinking it's a little like this: You're driving along. You're driving fast, but you can handle it. But at a certain point some road signs start appearing. Some are warnings—you know, the ones with red triangles. They're warning you of what might happen: You won't make it in time. Others are mostly unpleasant, like how you're feeling in your body. Are they also warning you about something, would you say?

Catherine: No, they're mostly just unpleasant. Although… It can't carry on like this. What will next week be like? I'm supposed to take a day off to take my son to some competition he's in. How am I going to fit that in?

Therapist: So there's that warning sign again: *You won't make it in time!*

Catherine: Right.

Therapist: I almost get the impression that there's another kind of sign—an order sign, you could say—one of those round ones: *Speed up!*

Catherine: *(silent at first)* I don't mean to speed up—it just happens. That's just what it's like.

Therapist: Exactly. As if it's automatic. I think a lot of signs are like that. We're so used to them that we hardly notice them. But still we obey them.

Catherine: *(slowly, tentatively)* You think I speed up?

Therapist: I thought that's what you said. You said you'd skip lunch. Just plug away.

Catherine: But what can I do? I can't just take things easy, that'd be impossible.

Therapist: Maybe. My point in this situation isn't that you have to do something else, whatever that would be. All I'm

saying is that we should see what's happening here. And
it seems to be that in certain situations road signs start
to appear. Some are warnings and they're clear. But
others are more subtle, more self-evident somehow, and
order you to accelerate. And you just do as the signs say.

In situations like this, what often happens is that the client starts to understand the connections but is unable to see the available options, as indicated
by Catherine above when she asks, "What can I do?" The therapist must then,
rather than just give advice, take her client through the connections that
present themselves in the current strategy. This can be a good time to link
back to the connection between what the client does and the consequences of
this—the connection, in other words, between B and C. Back to Catherine:

Catherine: So what can I do?

Therapist: I don't really know. We might be in a situation where it's
not so easy for either of us to see your options. There's
one thing that you have immediate experience of,
however, and that's what happens when you follow these
road signs. Maybe this experience is worth heeding, even
if we can't see any other alternative at the moment.

The pop-up and road-sign metaphors focus on the client's subsequent
behavior. It is the content of the pop-ups that induces Barry to act the way he
does, and it is the message on the signs that urges Catherine to speed up.
These connections are essential to the functional analysis, especially if one
believes that experiential avoidance and our interaction with our own spontaneously aroused responses is a key process in the development of psychological
problems. But as I pointed out in the connection between behavior and consequence (B and C), it can be important in the therapeutic dialogue to use metaphorical talk that is more open, and to invite self-examination by the client
rather than simply make assertions. This also applies to the A-B connection.
Catherine again:

Catherine: The stress is killing me. Never having time, running
around like a headless chicken. With my heart racing…

Therapist: This feeling of stress and the experience of never having enough time, your heart rate and so on. Have—do you have any notion of how it might vary?

Catherine: Yes, it comes and goes, of course. And mostly at work, with some days worse than others. Although recently it's been worse and more frequent.

Therapist: Let's say that I had a red light on this table (pointing to a table by her chair), like an alarm, you know? And I send you off with a little gadget that you carry around and that senses your stress levels, your feeling of not making it, your heart rate. And as soon as you start getting stressed, the lamp here starts flashing. What would happen, do you think? Would it flash at a regular rate or would it fluctuate a lot? Would the flashing mechanism break down so it just stood there giving off a constant red light?

Catherine: It would fluctuate a lot.

Therapist: What would it have looked like yesterday, say?

Yet again, the therapist uses a metaphor that conceivably fulfils our three conditions. The distress that Catherine reports is assumed to be functionally relevant to her problem. The source of the metaphor (the flashing alarm) is something that switches on and off, in much the same way as Catherine's emotional state does, by her own account. It alerts to danger, and does so in a way that is even more concrete than in the metaphor's target (Catherine's feelings of stress and the concomitant spontaneous thoughts). The connection with what Catherine does is not in focus; the main point of the metaphor is to help Catherine observe her own experience from a slightly new angle. A number of follow-up questions can be asked to develop this, provided that the therapist judges the metaphor to be meaningful to Catherine. For example:

Does the lamp ever come on and then go off again suddenly?

Does the light gradually go from weak to strong, or can it suddenly start flashing madly without warning?

Of the different things you notice with yourself when the lamp starts flashing, is there one thing that often precedes everything else?

Are there any situations at work that are always flash-free? Or any situations that virtually always cause the lamp to start flashing?

Within the compass of this metaphor, the therapist can also start to place ever greater stress on what Catherine does (B, in the functional analysis).

Would you say that you act in a certain way when the lamp flashes to turn it off?

When the lamp goes on, what do you tend to do then?

To help Catherine develop her faculty for self-observation, the therapist can construct home assignments whereby Catherine has to record "when the lamp goes on" between her sessions with the therapist. She might be asked to record different levels of "flash" or focus on recording what she does as a consequence of the "light going on."

When describing the three clinical principles or therapeutic strategies that are to guide therapeutic work (chapter 7), I made the point that the boundaries between them were somewhat blurred. This means that when we now, in a sense, leave the first principle (functional analysis) and move on to the second (establishing an observational distance from one's own responses), it is really an extension of the functional analysis. The second principle is, as it were, built into the functional analysis, but will now be developed with a particular focus.

CHAPTER 9

Creating Metaphors to Establish Observational Distance

As described in chapter 7, psychological rigidity, understood with the help of relational frame theory, means that we end up trapped in a vicious circle in our interactions with our own responses. These serve as "self-rules," which, when obeyed, whether knowingly or not, can induce dysfunctional action and leave us unable to extract ourselves from the rut into which we fall. (Törneke, Luciano, & Valdivia-Salas, 2008). This rigidity stems from our social learning experience and is perpetuated by the social context in which we live. A common consequence of this is the behavioral strategy known as experiential avoidance, by which we try to rid ourselves of spontaneously aroused feelings, memories, thoughts, and physical sensations in a way that is unproductive (Hayes et al., 1996). Our reactions influence us in a problematic way that precludes other, more efficient and purposeful behavioral strategies.

Such problems can be diminished with training in psychological flexibility, which crucially involves establishing an observational distance from our own responses—an experiential distance between ourselves as acting beings and everything we can observe in ourselves. *The problem is not what we feel, remember, think, or physically sense.* Indeed, these reactions are a product of our past and are potentially useful, even if they can be extremely painful in themselves. Naturally, many feelings, thoughts, and memories can be such that we would very much rather not experience them; but since we are powerless to change our past, any battle with spontaneously triggered reactions easily becomes counterproductive. The problem now is what we might be lured into doing when these reactions are aroused. By changing our way of interacting with these responses, we can, in lieu of actually eradicating them, modify the effect they have on the rest of our behavior. To be more precise, and in the language of RFT: we are to train ourselves in the ability to frame our own responses in hierarchy with deictic I (see chapter 7) and thus increase the chances that the rest of our behavior will change.

This training began already in the previous chapter under the heading Functional Analysis. Using metaphors occupies a key position in this work. In everyday speech, which includes a number of conventionalized or frozen metaphors, we also use external, material things to talk about our own subtle responses, such as emotions (see chapter 1). In the description in chapter 8 of doing a functional analysis, this is made more deliberate and pointed. Talking about physical sensations, feelings, and thoughts in the form of pop-ups, road signs, and red lamps is to talk about them in terms of objects that are remote from ourselves. This remoteness, however, does not apply in the same way to our own feelings and thoughts, as they are part of our own responding. At the same time, there is a definite *experiential* distance, a difference we experience between what we can observe in ourselves (what we feel, sense, think) and ourselves as the observer. According to RFT, the basis of this aptitude for experiencing ourselves as more than what we are feeling, sensing, remembering, or thinking at any given moment is our learned ability to frame our own responses in hierarchy with the deictic I (Törneke et al., 2016). Our ability to derive help from this in difficult situations is well known far outside the realm of psychotherapy. Who has not heard (or even said) the following comment after a sudden outburst of pent-up thoughts or emotions: "It's so good to get that off my chest."

This second principle of change work thus deepens an important aspect of what was started in the first.

Let us return to a clinical dialogue to illustrate how metaphors can be used for this. Perhaps the best known and possibly even most widely used metaphor in ACT, the "bus metaphor" (Hayes, Strosahl, & Wilson, 2012), is excellent for this purpose and opens the following dialogue with Andrew. Andrew is tormented by memories of sexual abuse when he was a boy and finds it almost impossible to socialize with others, an impediment that seems closely associated with overwhelming and almost ubiquitous self-critical thoughts.

> *Therapist:* We're all driving around in our own bus. And with us on board are lots of passengers: feelings we feel, thoughts we think, and memories we remember. We're driving the bus

and our passengers have boarded at different times, some of them we know when, others we have no idea. A simple example for me is that since I grew up in New York I've got a lot of passengers that are memories of New York. They often stand up at the back of the bus, even though I don't live there any more. Most of these New York passengers are fairly neutral, some are pleasant, but some are nasty. Do you have any New York passengers?

Andrew: Yeah. I mean, I'm not from New York but, sure, I have memories from there.

Therapist: Just now, when I mentioned New York, what appeared in your mind?

Andrew: Central Park, actually. I was there at a meeting in the spring.

Therapist: Okay, typical passengers. The pleasant kind, or…?

Andrew: (*chuckles*) Yeah, they're not bad. It was nice there, I suppose.

Therapist: But there are other passengers that aren't so pleasant, aren't there? Like the memories of what your neighbor did to you when you were little. Or those thoughts you have that there's something wrong with you, that you're not normal?

Andrew: That's exactly it. I'm not like others, so there must be something wrong. I've been aware of that pretty much for as long as I can remember. I get weird as soon as I'm in a group.

Therapist: So it's an old passenger, who's been on the bus for almost as long as you can remember.

Andrew: He's always there, more or less.

Therapist: What does he say to you?

Andrew: That there's something wrong with me, that I'm not right. That it's too late to do anything about it. That I'm simply damaged.

Therapist: How does it feel to hear all this?

Andrew: (*getting noticeably upset*) Terrible. Desperate. Sad and repulsive too, somehow.

Therapist: So it's really not just one passenger but a whole gang of them. Some say things to you, like there's something wrong with you, that you're damaged. Some passengers are feelings, such as repulsion and sorrow.

Andrew: I'm the repulsive one.

Therapist: A real pain of a passenger, that…

Andrew: It feels as if it's me.

Therapist: Yes, I can see that. He's standing next to you, leaning on your shoulder. I'd like to ask you one thing: Who notices all this? Who can hear what he says, that there's something wrong with you?

Andrew: (*a bit confused*) Me, I suppose…?

Therapist: Exactly. And who is it that feels the repulsion, the sorrow?

Andrew: That's me too.

Therapist: Now tell me, who's driving the bus?

The bus metaphor is one with a broad range of applications and that in many ways includes the possibility of working with all aspects of psychological flexibility (Hayes, Strosahl, & Wilson, 2012). If, for example, the therapist wants to use it to place the focus on her client's behavior, given the feelings and thoughts that appear, she can ask what the client does when his passengers talk to him. The dialogue can then be used for what was described under the functional analysis above. But now I would like to emphasize how the metaphor can be used to establish an observational distance; how to help Andrew make use of his ability to observe what is going on with him from the vantage point of "deictic I" so that his own feelings, thoughts, and other reactions lose some of their problematic influence on the rest of his behavior.

When the client's own reactions have a powerful, controlling influence over a wide span of his life, it is reasonable to expect them to do so during the interaction with the therapist as well. This can be an opportunity for the therapist to "strike while the iron is hot," so to speak.

Andrew: It's like this. There's something wrong with me. I see that all the time.

Therapist: Here too? While you're sitting here talking to me? Do you notice it here?

Andrew: Well I guess it's not so strong here, not right now. Being here's a bit special, isn't it? But, sure, I know that something's wrong now, as well.

Therapist: So your passengers are speaking to you here and now, albeit not as loudly as normal? They only vary in how loudly they speak, or perhaps how close they come?

Andrew: You could say that, yes.

Therapist: And who notices the difference? Who notices how loudly they shout or how close they get?

Andrew: Me.

Therapist: And right here and now: who's driving the bus?

To a therapist who believes that Andrew's problem is primarily logical in nature, the above reversion to the same issues might appear odd: if he needs, in the first instance, to "understand," he has surely already done so. But to a therapist who sees, from a learning-theory perspective, her job as being one of training, the reversion to the same principle is perfectly consistent. Both psychological rigidity and psychological flexibility are complex behavioral repertoires, and change is very much effected through training; it is this kind of training that therapy is to offer.

Another metaphor for the same principle is the "suggestion box," which is especially useful when the private or subtle responses affecting the client are imperative in tone and dictate what he is to do. Since rule-governed behavior, compliance with self-instructions, is such a dominant part of the human repertoire, most rapid private responses have a kind of advisory or warning function, which is sometimes more distinct. Let us return to Catherine from the museum:

Therapist: It's about having time to get things done, plugging away.

Catherine: Yes, that's how it feels in these situations. I just don't know how to get rid of it.

Therapist: No. And when you're stressed and under pressure, as you are, it's completely understandable that you want to rid yourself of what you're experiencing. The feeling, the physical stress, and all the thoughts about what you have to do...

Catherine: That's what I'm trying to do, to stay calm. But it's not working.

Therapist: I guess that's an important observation. Making sure that you stay calm when you're already stressed and upset is pretty hard. But what if you don't have to get rid of it there and then, don't have to struggle to stay calm? What if there's another way once you're there? Another way of dealing with that feeling and all those thoughts pressing on you.

Catherine: How do you mean?

Therapist: What if our spontaneous feelings and thoughts are a kind of suggestion box. You know, the kind you find in offices or public buildings. Do you have one of those at work?

Catherine: Yes, but not for us. Only for visitors to the museum.

Therapist: Okay, and what does it look like?

Catherine: It's blue, wooden. Kind of nice.

Therapist: I think that in some way we all walk around with our own suggestion box; all the thoughts and feelings we get. It's a good thing, because we get lots of tips. Nothing wrong with the box; it's doing its job. It's a good idea to read what gets put in it. But you don't have to do everything the notes say. You can read one, put it back in the box, and make your own choice about whether or not to do what it said. You're more than just your suggestion box, so to speak.

If the therapist has the impression that the metaphor is meaningful to Catherine, it can be used to devise a home assignment for her.

Therapist: I'm going to give you a suggestion box to take back with you, which you can use until our next session.

Catherine: Er, okay...?

Therapist: An imaginary one, that is. You said you liked the one you have at the museum. Imagine it looks like that. Change the color if you like, to make it your very own. *(Trying to give the metaphor's source concrete features.)*

Catherine: Okay. Red, then.

Therapist: Can you picture it?

Catherine: Sure.

Therapist: Now I'd like you to use this red box. When you feel that sense of stress making you want to get things done, making you plug away, read the suggestion and put it back in the box.

Catherine: And stop stressing?

Therapist: At this stage you don't have to make any effort to change anything. If you push yourself, so be it. If you speed up, you speed up. All I want is for you to note

when a suggestion gets put in the box, read it, and put it
back. There's lots of room in your box, so it can take
many suggestions. We'll look at them next week. See if
there are any new ones or if they're all just old,
hackneyed suggestions.

Another example of the same principle is the following dialogue with
Andrew.

Therapist: If all this that you've told me, everything that's
               happened and everything it makes you feel and think,
               were a book, what would be the title?

Andrew: "The Repulsive Failure." Shit!

Therapist: A pretty brutal title. A lot of pain there…

Andrew: (sighs) Yep.

Therapist: (taking down a book from her shelf and holding it out) Like
               this one. "The Repulsive Failure." Lots of chapters, some
               old, others more recently written (flicking through the
               book). I'd say there are different ways of approaching a
               book like this. You can lose yourself in it, give it all your
               attention, get really absorbed (holding the book in front of
               her face, turning the pages eagerly). Or you can keep it at
               arm's length, try hard not to look at it (holding the book
               as far away from herself as possible and trying to avert her
               eyes). Both ways are understandable and natural. The
               book seems important, and it's painful to read. These
               two strategies are in many ways different but they have
               one problem in common. Both demand your attention
               and get in the way of other things. In both these cases
               (illustrating both again) my ability to talk to you, here and
               now, for example, is interfered with (illustrating how the
               book and the two ways of dealing with it obstruct eye
               contact and dialogue, then falling silent to check that
               Andrew perceives what she has said as meaningful).

Andrew: I guess so. I guess I've got my nose in the book most of the time. I try to hold it away from me in some sense too, but I rarely manage it. It blocks out almost everything, I think. Is there any alternative?

Therapist: *(holding the book to one side, in view, and turning her gaze to Andrew as during a normal conversation)* I'm thinking that this is what we're practicing here. Having the book with you—after all, it's not going away anyhow. Having it at an observational distance. Here am I and there is the book *(touching and raising the book)*. And I can turn my attention to something important, such as the conversation with you even if I'm fully aware that the book's here *(touching it again)*. "The Repulsive Failure." And I am more than just my book.

Once again, the entire metaphorical dialogue is dependent on three basic conditions if it is to be of any use to Andrew.

1.   The metaphor's target (Andrew's experience of self-criticism and repulsion, his painful memories, and what he does in their presence) must be functionally important—in other words, part of Andrew's problem.

2.   The metaphor's source must correspond to central parts of its target. In this case, Andrew must recognize his experience of struggling with his own thoughts, feelings, and memories in the description of how one interacts with the book.

3.   The metaphor's source must embody a property or function that is more salient there than it is in its target. The main thing in this case is that the book is distinct from the person interacting with it, even though it is a kind of biography, and that Andrew can act independently of it. This distinction is clearer in terms of the book than it is of his own spontaneously triggered responses. But the very point of using the metaphor is to enhance Andrew's ability to establish this distinction, this observational distance from his own feelings and thoughts.

In the above example, it is the therapist who acts with the book and uses it to, metaphorically, illustrate a point to her client. This can be developed so that the client is invited to take active part in similar exercises. I will be returning to this in chapter 13, and to how metaphors and experiential exercises can act synergistically in therapeutic work.

This final dialogue with Andrew also touches, again metaphorically, on the third principle of therapy: that the therapist is to help her client connect with what is important to him and to take concrete steps in that direction. This is yet further illustration that these three strategies for change are not completely distinct from each other. The ability to articulate what is important for you as a person and to set a course accordingly depends on your ability to establish an observational distance from your own responses. You need to be able to observe things in yourself, what you feel and what you think, in order to be able to reach a meaningful decision about what is important in your own life.

CHAPTER 10

Creating Metaphors to Clarify Direction

One characteristic human trait that sets us apart from all other animals is our flexible ability to choose. We often do things that have no short-term payoff, and even things that are painful, provided we perceive them as meaningful. We go to the dentist so that we can keep our teeth; we turn down an evening out with friends to study for an exam; we get up and change our baby's diaper in the middle of the night despite having not slept properly for weeks; and we rummage around in our bins to recycle our trash. None of this is anything we *must* do. But we *can* do it. And can *not* do it. We call this the ability *to choose* and it is central to us as humans and to what we have discussed as psychological flexibility.

Let me take another metaphor from ACT (Hayes, Strosahl, & Wilson, 2012) to illustrate this point:

Therapist: Is it important to you that everyone wear blue socks?

Barry: What? Of course not!

Therapist: Try to feel that it's important.

Barry: I can't. It's impossible. What a strange question! Do you think it's important?

Therapist: No, and I can't make myself feel that, no matter how hard I try. But listen to this: You and I could agree that it's important. We could make sure to act as if it were a matter of life and death. We could buy lots of blue socks and hand them out to people on the street.

Barry:	That's madness!
Therapist:	Isn't it? My point is, though, that we could. Couldn't we?
Barry:	Sure we could.
Therapist:	What else could we do if we assumed it was really important that everyone wore blue socks?
Barry:	Advertise. We could pay celebrities to always show themselves wearing blue socks. Start some kind of Facebook campaign, perhaps.
Therapist:	Exactly. Collect all other kinds of socks we could get our hands on and light a big bonfire. All this we could do, even though we don't really think wearing blue socks is important at all. But what's stopping us then, what's stopping you, from directing yourself toward something that you do actually think is really, genuinely important?

Here, the therapist uses Barry's immediate experience in the dialogue (his insight that he could act on the basis of the importance of blue-sock wearing) as the metaphor's source, and the opportunity to set a course for something he really does think is important as its target. The same conditions must apply once more if the metaphor is to be of help to Barry:

1. The metaphor's target (the ability to set a course toward something important) must in itself be important in the change work with Barry.

2. The metaphor's source must correspond to central parts of its target. In this case, Barry must recognize his experience of choosing in the slightly ridiculous example of blue socks.

3. The metaphor's source must embody a property or function that is more salient there than it is in its target. Pivotal to this case is how the insight that Barry could choose to act in accordance with something to which he puts no value brings clarity to the possibility of acting in the direction of something he genuinely thinks is

important, which was less salient to Barry before the metaphor was uttered. The point of using the metaphor is to increase the likelihood that Barry will take a step toward things that are important to him.

The point of directing the conversation to something that the client values rather than merely focusing on problems and difficulties is, of course, that it can motivate the client to effect change. In our review of functional analysis, I stressed that human beings are affected by the consequences of their behavior. What we get back from what we do affects what we will do in the future. But from what we have learned about relational framing, we also know that an aspect of this is that we are sense-making creatures. We can visualize consequences, even those of which we do not yet have any immediate experience. If these "consequences" are desired, we can plot out a course in that direction, even if it means passing through a patch of troubled waters ahead. And this is exactly what is needed in change work, since change often causes discomfort, at least in the short term. The more difficult the change needed, the more we get from connecting with what we value.

I mentioned earlier that the bus metaphor can be used to work with all three principles of enhancing psychological flexibility. After having been used in the first instance to increase the chances of the client establishing an observational distance from his own thoughts and feelings, the dialogue can continue:

Therapist: If you were free to drive wherever you wanted, if all these frightening and disruptive passengers lost their power over you, in what direction would you take your bus?

The "life is a journey" metaphor is very evident here, and is integrated into many of the other metaphors that have been used in the dialogues I have reproduced. The therapist can ask Barry where he would like to drive if he no longer felt the need to park. With Catherine, she could talk about a journey along which all road signs had lost their influence.

Therapist: If you entered a road that didn't have loads of signs telling you this and that, do you have any idea what direction would be of importance to you?

Things we value are associated with emotions. When we are happy, sad, scared, or disgusted, when we feel ashamed or curious, that is when something touches us. That thing, at least for the moment, is important to us. There is reason therefore to be attentive and to seek out emotional reactions in the client, including with questions about what he finds important. Not everything felt at the moment of speaking is important in the general sense we are discussing now, but emotions flag the areas on which we can concentrate. There is also a danger that answers to questions about "the important things in life" will be conventional and "correct." However, in that we are on a quest for concrete motivators, we are seeking something that touches the client.

One way of finding these triggers is to ask about concrete situations, no matter how mundane they might seem. People who find it hard to talk about what they value and who answer "I don't know" are also, of course, sensemaking creatures, so the therapist can assume that the important things are there somewhere, no matter how well concealed. Human action always has a purpose, and in the search for relevant concrete and affecting situations, metaphors can prove very useful.

> *Therapist:*   I'm wondering something. Let's say that I had a new pill that caused no side effects and that made you completely free. Free to do whatever you want. But there's a catch. It's very expensive, so you can only get one per week. And it also lasts only five or six hours. If you were to take this pill over the next few weeks or months, do you have any idea when you'd take it?
>
> *Andrew:*   *(silent at first)* Tricky. Five or six hours isn't that long. But maybe Thursday evenings, in fact.
>
> *Therapist:*   Okay, Thursday evenings. What happens then?
>
> *Andrew:*   I saw they had a choir for people who want to sing but who aren't experienced. They practice on Thursday evenings, in the church. I've been trying to pluck up the courage to go.
>
> *Therapist:*   What attracts you to it?

Andrew: I've always liked singing. But it's not just that. It's about doing something with other people, feeling that I belong.

Therapist: It sounds as if we've hit on something important here, something that means something to you.

Once the dialogue has reached this point, it can be taken to a deeper level through Andrew's experience. We will return to this kind of focus in the next chapter.

The pill metaphor can, of course, be adapted to many different situations and clients. And its effect can vary…

Another metaphorical question is as follows:

Therapist: Let's assume that your life, so far, is a modern TV series. You know, one of those that run in seasons. If I understand right, sometimes they change scriptwriters from one season to the next. Imagine that now you've been given the chance to take over the script of your own life. You can't change what's already happened, as the series has led up to this day. And there are some instructions you have to stick to. This is an everyday, somewhat realistic series, so you can't insert any weird sci-fi stuff or anything. Nothing magic. You, the main character, also have to do well—maybe not with everything, but with the important things. Even if the series hasn't been like this, the point is now for it to have that "feel-good factor." You can be the person you want to be. Can you say something about the upcoming episode and how the main character will behave?

As the reader might have noticed, the metaphor veers a little toward the imaginative here. A scenario is set up and the client is asked to imagine himself in it. This is related to the way the therapist deliberately tries to seek the source of the metaphor in the client's experience here and now to then relate it to the metaphor's target, namely the question of what is important to the client in his own life, and what steps can be taken in that direction. This brings us closer to what we will be devoting ourselves to in chapter 13, namely the interaction between metaphors and experiential exercises.

It can be valuable to distinguish between this way of taking direction on one hand and defining goals on the other, as the end point of a journey can easily appear too remote to be motivating.

Therapist: When we talk about setting a course for something important, there's one thing I think can be important— the difference between direction and a goal, or direction and outcome. To take a simple example: where are you going after our meeting today?

Andrew: Into town to do some shopping.

Therapist: And I daresay it's very likely that you'll do just that. But isn't it the case that strictly speaking, you can't actually be certain you'll make it. Something else might happen, something unforeseen. You might get run over and be rushed to hospital, or you might get a phone call that makes you change your plans.

Andrew: Sure, that's possible.

Therapist: We have no guarantees that we'll reach our goals or of the outcome of what we do. Hopefully we'll reach whatever goals we set up, but we can never know for sure. But there is something you can know at this moment, something that is completely up to you.

Andrew: And that is?

Therapist: Well, when you walk out of here, even the first steps you take toward the door here, in a sense they are directed toward town, right? The direction you take is up to you, at any moment in time. You can change it as you go, but it's your choice, all the time.

Here the therapist tries to use Andrew's experience of one area (the action of directing his steps) as a source for affecting the metaphor's target, namely what it would be like for the client to direct his actions toward things that he imbues with long-term meaning. The point is to encourage the act of taking direction in the here and now without being blocked by a goal that seems too far away to reach.

A decisive moment in all therapeutic work is when actual, concrete steps are taken, for it is only then that the client can connect with new consequences. This rather self-evident point can also be made with a simple metaphor:

Andrew: I don't know, I don't think I can. All my thoughts and feelings are spinning around my head. I can't sort them out.

Therapist: We sometimes get into situations where our head isn't a friend, and all we can rely on is our feet. It's where you place your foot that you leave a footprint.

In the introduction to chapter 8, I pointed out that my initial emphasis would be on the therapist's active and conscious use of metaphors. However, most metaphors in everyday dialogue, including in psychotherapeutic conversations, are not "contrived" but spontaneous. Just how we catch and use these kinds of metaphors is what we will turn to next.

CHAPTER 11

Catching Metaphors

One of the most obvious conclusions of modern metaphor research is that "metaphors are everywhere." They are the building blocks of language and many have already been embedded (!) in just these first couple of sentences. See how many you can spot! (Catching, re-search, building blocks…)

Even human behavior not traditionally considered verbal (such as gestures) often seems to derive from metaphors and analogies. RFT can provide a relatively simple explanation for this: we learn from childhood a specific skill that enables us to relate phenomena to each other independently of their properties. We relate them on the basis of arbitrary contextual cues and can therefore, in principle, place anything in relation to anything else in any possible way. When we relate relations in a certain way we produce metaphors (see chapter 4).

Thus metaphors can be found wherever humans act. And our way of relating, of "metaphorizing," is an integral part of almost everything we do. It likely follows that how we use metaphors, often unwittingly, says something about us, about how we see the world and ourselves. It says something about us and something about the likelihood of us acting in one way or another.

Some of these frozen or dead metaphors possibly have little to tell; but as linguists have shown us, they are often more alive than we might think (see chapters 1 and 2).

Let us take as an example the title of this chapter—"catching" metaphors. This is not a "contrived" metaphor, but one that spontaneously popped into my head as I was trying to come up with a possible heading. It is relatively conventional and well-established. But one might well ask: does my choice of word say something about me? Perhaps something about my way of looking at or practicing psychotherapy? Does it say anything important, if, that is, someone were to examine my way of doing psychotherapy more closely?

Maybe, maybe not. But anyone who wanted to find out (as part of a functional analysis of my therapeutic conduct, for example) could ask a question. Let me suggest one:

That, catching metaphors, what kind of catching is that?

If I were to attempt an answer to that question, I would have to develop the relational network that the word "catching" constitutes for me in this context. More simply: I would have to say something more of what I meant. If this metaphor, when spoken or written, were "frozen" or "dead," any attempt by me to answer the question might "bring it back to life" (see chapter 2). Maybe I would observe something about my way of doing psychotherapy that, before I tried to answer, was not particularly clear to me. Maybe. Maybe not. I return, again, to the three essential conditions.

1. The metaphor's target (my way of doing psychotherapy) must be functionally important—in other words, there has to be a reason for me to look at this particular aspect of my behavior. If this way of acting is therapeutically helpful, maybe I should do it more; if it is not, maybe I should do it less.

2. The metaphor's source ("to catch") must correspond to central parts of its target. In this case, I must recognize something in the expression that reminds me of how I work as a psychotherapist. Since I was the one using the metaphor, it is reasonable to suppose that such is the case.

3. The metaphor's source must embody a property or function that is more salient there than it is in its target. The main thing in this case is that the word "catch" must clarify to me what I tend to do. If it is then something that I should change (do more or less of) is a question upon which my analysis has not yet touched.

Back to the Three Strategies

A central thesis of this chapter—of this entire book, in fact—is that our way of using metaphors (dead or alive) contains important information about who we are, how we tend to act, and how we will probably act in the future. There is thus potentially vital information here for a functional analysis. However, it must be pointed out that this does not mean that all metaphorical speech is of equal therapeutic value. What I am advocating is not some general "metaphor therapy." Even when capturing spontaneously surfacing metaphors, the therapist does this on the basis of the three strategic principles described before: functional analysis, establishing an observational distance, and clarifying direction. We adhere to the conclusion from metaphor research that opened the clinical section of this book, namely that it is not enough to focus on metaphors; we must also focus on relevant clinical processes.

In this context, it might be worth mentioning some of the therapeutic models that stand out for their focus on metaphors, and especially their examination of those used by clients. These models lie beyond what is normally referred to as the evidence-based tradition, but are relatively well known, and are probably encountered if one actively seeks information on psychotherapy and metaphors. One example is metaphor therapy (Kopp, 1995; Kopp & Craw, 1998); another is clean language (Lawley & Tompkins, 2000; Sullivan & Rees, 2008). While these models are mutually different, they all lay the emphasis on the metaphors used by the client and contain concrete manuals giving precise instructions on how to ask questions in interaction with the client. Even if one, from the premises of this book, has reason to be skeptical about parts of those models (especially in clean language, which makes rather grandiose claims), it is nonetheless interesting to note that some of the practical advice given in those approaches tallies with what seems reasonable in terms of modern linguistic metaphor research and behavior analysis (including RFT). So if the reader is familiar with these models, she will recognize some of what follows.

Part of the evidence-based tradition that has things to contribute to the work to be described in this chapter is the therapeutic models that are often classified as "emotion focused" (Angus & Greenberg, 2011; Greenberg & Pavio, 1997; Greenberg, Rice & Elliot, 1993). Characteristic of these models is their emphasis on heeding the client's reactions at the moment of interaction with the therapist. This has specific significance with regard to listening attentively to the relevant metaphors the client uses, and general significance with regard to using relevant sequences guided by the three principal therapeutic strategies.

Catching Metaphors for Functional Analysis

Andrew describes his experience of a social situation.

Andrew: It's like I'm an ant.

Let us assume that the therapist takes this to be a metaphor of possible significance and usefulness, and so "catches" this metaphorical expression. This she does by making a comment or asking a question, the actual wording of which is determined by where she wishes to focus attention. Let us assume that she just wants Andrew to develop what he has just said, that which might be a relevant source for a metaphor whose target is an aspect of how he experiences his situation. In RFT terms: the therapist wants Andrew to describe the network that constitutes the metaphor's source.

Therapist: An ant? What kind of ant?

Andrew: A tiny, trembling ant.

Therapist: And what's it like to be a tiny, trembling ant?

Andrew: Not nice. I feel so small and insignificant. And frightened.

Here, the therapist shifts the focus from the metaphor's source (having first asked Andrew to develop it) to its target (what it is about his experience that he relates to "being an ant"), and Andrew replies by describing how he feels. But it is not inconceivable that he could have given a different answer:

Therapist: And what's it like to be a tiny, trembling ant?

Andrew: I just try to make myself even smaller so that no one sees me.

Here, Andrew answers the therapist's question by describing what he does, not primarily how he feels. Since the therapist is working along the lines of her basic strategy—to perform a functional analysis—the difference between these replies is relevant. When Andrew talks about what he does, he talks about B in a functional analysis. When talking about how he feels, this is, from the therapist's perspective, part of the circumstances under which Andrew does what he does: in other words, A in a functional analysis. Both are of course relevant. If Andrew spontaneously describes how it feels, the therapist will probably eventually ask:

> "And when you feel tiny like that, insignificant and frightened,
> what do you do?"

Here, from the description of A, the therapist is seeking B in the hope of clarifying the A–B relationship.

When Andrew gives the second answer and describes how he acts (B), he actually includes a key aspect of the circumstances (A) that precede (antecede) his attempt to make himself "even smaller." He says:

> "I just try to make myself even smaller so that no one sees me."

That "no one sees me" is a desired consequence, but in the functional analysis it is a circumstance under which he makes himself "even smaller," which is to say an aspect of A. It is a response that arises in a certain social situation, and Andrew interacts with this, his own response, by trying to make himself "even smaller." If the therapist wishes to explore this relationship in order to see, for example, if it can be of general relevance, she can ask:

> "You don't want anyone to see you, so you try to make yourself even
> smaller. Is this, this feeling tiny and scared and wanting no one to see
> you and your trying to make yourself even smaller, something you
> recognize from other situations?"

If she also wants to clarify the relationship between B and C, the conversation could go like this:

> *Andrew:*   Yes, it's pretty typical. I feel so small and useless so I just
>   try to make myself even smaller so that no one can see
>   me, see what I'm like.
>
> *Therapist:* In your experience so far, how well does that work?

Here, the therapist is searching for the B-C link, that between the strategy Andrew applies and the outcome it produces.

As the reader might have noticed, the therapist uses the same strategy here as described in earlier chapters, although in those cases she was the creator of the metaphors. Here, she uses metaphors initiated by the client and tries to capture them with her questions. The rationale for this is simple: if the client describes something that is central to his problem using a metaphor, then the metaphor probably contains useful information. At the same time, the three previously described conditions for a helpful clinical metaphor still apply. And the most important thing is this: the metaphor must concern something of clinical/functional relevance to the client's problem. Therefore, this is not work that merely focuses spontaneously aroused metaphors in general. The therapist directs attention to metaphors that are useful in working according to the three principles of change. And the most basic one is doing a functional analysis.

I stressed above, when describing the therapeutic dialogue with Andrew, that subtle differences in the questions asked and responses given shift the focus onto one or another part of the A–B–C functional analysis. The therapist must be clear in her mind about these differences—in other words, she must know what she is asking for and learn to make these distinctions. This said, there is no prescribed order or manner in which this is to be done, and there is no empirical evidence to suggest a preference. The task is simply to identify the A–B–C sequence with the aim of helping the client discern his own behavior and thereby change what he wants to change. Catching metaphors for this purpose is a useful strategy.

Let me take another example. In the dialogue with Catherine, she describes again her feelings of stress at work, and how they totally overwhelm her.

> *Catherine:* I just don't know what else I can do, how I can go about changing things. It feels so completely out of my control. It all just comes pouring into me. (*And with greater emphasis*): Shouldn't the fontanelle have closed up by now?[7]

The metaphorical question about her fontanelle is hardly conventional. The advantage of the client coining a new metaphor like this is that the therapist can assume that something important is being said. The conversation is about something central to the client's problem and the client describes some aspect of this with the help of a "living" metaphor. Thus are our three conditions for a functional clinical metaphor fulfilled:

---

7   With gratitude to the client who once used this very metaphor under different circumstances.

1. The metaphor's target must be functionally important. In this instance, it might be unclear to the therapist exactly what the metaphor's target is. In other words, what does Catherine mean with her talk of her fontanelle? Since the conversation is about the distress she experiences in her problem situations, it is very likely that the aspect of them that she describes in this way (the metaphor's target) is relevant. Clarifying what is referred to is one of the therapist's tasks in the ensuing dialogue.

2. The metaphor's source must correspond to central parts of its target. Since Catherine uses the metaphor, we can assume that this condition is fulfilled—for her, if not the therapist. If the therapist needs clarification, she can ask questions that help Catherine describe the relational network that constitutes a "fontanelle that has not closed up."

3. The metaphor's source must embody a property or function that is more salient there than it is in its target. Again, since Catherine chooses this way of expressing something she wants to describe, we can assume that this condition is fulfilled. For Catherine, the metaphor's source (what she says about the fontanelle) contains a property that is clearer there than in the experience that she is trying to talk about in using it (the metaphor's target).

How should the therapist continue the dialogue? If we assume that in the first situation she fails to comprehend, there is room for some clarifying questions that can help Catherine develop the network:

Therapist: The fontanelle hasn't closed up? How hasn't it closed up?

Catherine: I don't know how, but it's as if it's open and everything's just pouring in. Straight in! I get hot, I get palpitations, and I get all wound up about having no time. I don't know what I can do to stop it.

Here we see that Catherine has understood the question "how?" as the therapist asking how it happened and not how she means. The question could possibly have been phrased better, but no matter. In the above, Catherine develops what she means anyway. Then the therapist can continue:

Therapist: To stop everything just pouring into the fontanelle?

Catherine: Exactly. (*Smiles a little.*) It's as if I should get it sewn up, you know?

Therapist: Do you try to do that, would you say? To sew it up?

Catherine: I don't know. I don't know how to. But sure, I try to put a stop to it.

Therapist: How? How do you try to put a stop to it?

Notice how the therapist on the one hand tries to keep Catherine in her own metaphor and develop the relational networks comprising it, and on the other fulfil her strategy to perform a functional analysis with her. What is clear in this dialogue is that the experience Catherine relates (the metaphor's target) is what the functional analysis would designate as A, in that she describes aspects of the circumstance under which she does what she does. And as we, for theoretical reasons (see chapter 7), have come to expect, her own spontanous responses (metaphorically: the experience of having an open fontanelle) are crucial to this.

In the dialogue, Catherine also addresses, again in the form of a metaphor, that which the functional analysis would designate B (what she does given the circumstances she experiences). She says that she "is trying to put a stop to things entering through her fontanelle," and that it should be "sewn up." Once an effective metaphor for some part of the A–B–C sequence has been introduced, either by the client or as in previous chapters by the therapist, it is often a relatively simple matter to develop it and talk about other parts of the functional sequence. If Catherine had stopped at simply saying she had experience of having an "open fontanelle," the therapist could have asked:

> "And when this happens, when the fontanelle is open and everything just pours through it, what do you do then?"

In a situation where the metaphor used by the client mainly seems to relate to the consequence of some clinically relevant behavior and the therapist wants to draw attention to earlier parts of the sequence, all she need do is ask what preceded it—perhaps in the form of a metaphor:

Catherine: It gets empty, completely empty. It doesn't matter what I do, it's completely empty.

Therapist: If we stay in this situation, when it's completely empty, and if we turn back time a little, to just before—what happens there?

Notice that the therapist can always take the conversation in different directions depending on what she deems relevant at any one point. When Catherine says that everything is empty, the therapist could have asked a more probing question designed to help Catherine develop the relational network "empty":

"It's completely empty. What kind of empty?"

Again, the important thing when deciding where to go in the functional analysis is not what is "right"; after all, the therapist rarely knows what that is. The important thing is to take different directions and for the therapist and the client together to evaluate what happens. The functional sequence A–B–C is a focus to which it is constantly worth returning.

In the episode above, when the therapist helps Catherine to hold onto and develop her metaphor, we see that Catherine gives a little smile as she describes something painful to her. What we are likely seeing here is a moment when the strategy of making a functional analysis already, to a degree, includes what is to be focused further in the next strategy: to establish an observational distance.

Catching Metaphors to Establish Observational Distance

When it comes to client-generated metaphors, there is more reason to assume they describe problems rather than solutions—at least early on in the therapeutic process. By definition, the client has more experience of the problem than he does of the solution; otherwise he would not have sought therapy in the first place. This means that this second strategy will often be dominated by therapist-generated metaphors. At the same time, the client's metaphors embody possibilities. Simply the fact that the client sets his own experience (the metaphor's target) in relation to something else, often an external object (the metaphor's source), creates an opportunity to train him in psychological flexibility and establish an observational distance (in RFT terms: to frame his own responses in hierarchy with the deictic I). When Andrew talks about his experience of being like a tiny trembling ant, the therapist can invite him to practice this particular ability by asking something like:

"What does the ant look like?"

"Who is it who's observing the ant right now?"

"If you touch the ant, how does it feel?"

She can also ask Andrew to imagine the ant's physical presence in the here and now, and to interact with it:

"Can you imagine the ant here in the room? Where do you want to put it? Can you move it further away? Bring it closer?"

In this way, the therapist can move on to strategies that we will be looking more closely at in chapter 13, namely how metaphor use can coact with experiential exercises.

Similarly, the therapist can work with Catherine's experience of having everything "pouring into her fontanelle." When Catherine develops the network that is the metaphor's source and describes different aspects of the metaphor's target (her experience), the therapist uses concrete properties of the former to talk about the latter:

Therapist: If you were to point to this fontanelle, where would it be?

Catherine: (running her hand over the top of her head, tugging at her hair) There, roughly.

Therapist: Can you show me roughly how big the hole is?

Catherine: (drawing a small circle on her head) Here. (Removes hand.)

Therapist: And who is it that notices the fontanelle and how it feels when everything pours into it?

Catherine: I do.

Therapist:	And who is it moving your hand?
Catherine:	Me.
Therapist:	Exactly. It's the fontanelle, it's the hand, and it's the one who notices everything and who moves the hand.

Once we understand the principle for what we are trying to achieve, what it is we are training, client-generated metaphors provide infinite possibilities for doing this. In the dialogue with Catherine, the following questions could also be asked:

"The stuff that pours into you, can you picture it? If so, what does it look like?"

"Where does it end up?"

"Where does it come from?"

Some of these questions might not be of much help; the client might not be able to answer them or might indicate in some other way that they are doing no good. So the therapist abandons this example, but returns with the same basic strategy in another situation, perhaps via a different metaphor. This method of establishing an observational distance in such a concrete way is perhaps the most special aspect of metaphor use as it is described in this book. Many might dismiss it as "woolly," especially if they fail to see the point of the strategy and its theoretical underpinnings. Remarkably few clients react in this way, however—at least in my experience.

Let us assume that Catherine finds the questions strange and instead of interacting as she does above, says something that indicates a slight breakdown of the client-therapist collaboration. What to say?

Therapist:	If you were to point to this fontanelle, where would it be?
Catherine:	(hesitant, wary) I mean, there is no fontanelle, I know that…
Therapist:	No, of course not. But this is a kind of game, like we are playing around. A serious way of playing, though, from my side. Would it be okay to carry on?

This dialogue brings to mind another question I often get asked when dealing with this approach as a supervisor or trainer: Should we explain what we're doing?

There is no real empirically based answer to this question. There are, however, some principles: If we are in the middle of exploring a spontaneously generated metaphor, we will lose the point if we suddenly step aside and explain it. Explanations are presumably most useful beforehand or afterward. Since our aim is to teach a skill rather than intellectual understanding, there is always a danger that explanatory talk will misdirect the focus and disrupt the training process. We have a natural tendency to exaggerate the importance of understanding when it comes to creating change. On the other hand, a small amount of explanation can make the client more willing to participate. In other experiential therapeutic situations, such as exposure, conscious processing is, as many leading scholars now agree, at its most valuable following a new experience (Craske et al., 2014). The same applies here. So if we want to explain in advance, we ought to keep it brief:

> "We can play around with this a bit. It might seem a bit odd but there's a point to it. Would that be okay?"

In the post-experience context, however, the needs are different. In some situations explaining is unnecessary as the client fully gets the relevance of an experience he has just effected. In others, however, subsequent explanation can have a consolidatory function. Here too I would advise you to keep it brief and to answer any questions the client might have. A possible comment could be:

> "The point is to practice a new approach. These are difficult, painful things we're talking about, situations in which how you feel and think or what you remember become obstacles to you in important areas of your life. What I'm trying to do is see if we can find ways for you to go forward, ways that work better for you."

This is the situation in which we can use the therapist-generated metaphor described in chapter 9, where the therapist illustrates establishing an observational distance by holding a book close to her face and then holding it away from her or placing it on the table beside her, and say something like:

"One thing we're practicing by doing this is establishing a kind of observational distance from what troubles you. Like with the book. So that you have more freedom of movement."

There are some relatively conventionalized metaphors that are relevant to this purpose and that, if employed by the client, can be caught for further development:

Client: It was nice to get all this off my chest. I've got no one else to talk to.

Therapist: Now that you've gotten it off your chest, where is it now, would you say?

Or another fairly common expression:

Client: I've got quite a lot of baggage.

Therapist: If we were to put your baggage out here on the floor, what would it look like?

Catching Metaphors to Clarify Direction

What is important to people can be found in an unexpected place: the locus of their pain. When we are struggling with something, when we are in pain, it is an indirect sign that something is important to us. Someone suffering from social anxiety places a value on social interaction—otherwise why would the risk of humiliation be a problem? Someone who is depressed is experiencing some form of loss, which is an oblique indication that he places a value on the object, physical or abstract, of which he has been deprived. And someone contemplating suicide is announcing that she values something, even if it is merely freedom from anguish.

Barry: I'm not getting anywhere. Things have just ground to a halt.

Therapist: If you look in that direction, where you are not getting, what do you see?

Barry:	A group of people. A group that I'm not in.
Therapist:	A group you're not in. Is it a group you want to be in?
Barry:	Of course is it. But it just seems so remote.
Therapist:	So it's like they're far away. Can you describe the group at a distance? What do you see?

The therapist can then ask different follow-up questions, such as:

"What are they doing? Do you recognize anyone in it? What part would you like to play in that group? Are there any other groups you'd like to join, if it were possible?"

All this is to give Barry a clearer experiential connection with what is important to him. If the dialogue around this seems fruitful, the therapist can ask questions that reconnect with the functional analysis, in terms of both what Barry does when "regarding something from afar" and what could be a possible alternative and a step toward what he himself deems to be important in his life. For example:

"If you were free to join this group, if you suddenly found yourself with them, what would you want to do? And: If you were to take some steps toward such a possibility, what kind of steps would they be?"

The last question assumes that Barry has already established an observational distance from the obstructive emotions of despondency that he has described, and from the thoughts and ideas related to them. Otherwise there is the risk that he would simply say that he cannot take those steps.

Catherine describes part of her problem with the metaphor "the fontanelle is open" and "everything is pouring in." The therapist can use this metaphor in a contrasting sense to search for something of importance to Catherine:

Therapist:	In these worst situations, it's as if the fontanelle is open and everything's falling through it. Are there any situations at work when it's more like the fontanelle's closed and you can do what you want?
Catherine:	Sometimes. More so before.

> *Therapist:*   When things don't fall through your fontanelle and you
>   can do what you want, either now or as it was before,
>   where does that come from?
>
> *Catherine:*   More from within me, maybe. *(She makes a circling
>   motion with her hand that starts at her chest and goes
>   forward, outward).*
>
> *Therapist:*   And when you can do things that come more from
>   within, what is it you want to do?
>
> *Catherine:*   *(a little hesitant, uncertain)* I don't know. Create
>   something. Build something.
>
> *Therapist:*   And when you want to build something at work, what
>   would you want to build?

In this case, the therapist catches a metaphor ("to build something"), which, unlike the "fontanelle" metaphor, could easily be seen as being very conventional and thus "frozen" or "dead." In terms of the basic theoretical outlook described earlier, this does not stop it from containing vital—and thus useful—information about what Catherine considers important. If Catherine replies in a way that confirms this, the therapist can follow up with questions that help her probe more deeply what this metaphor means to her, perhaps by asking about other areas of her life where she feels she "builds more as she wants," what she does in those circumstances, and what she could do at work that is oriented toward "building what she wants to build" rather than, as is often currently the case, toward "sewing up the fontanelle."

One way of capturing client-generated metaphors on the theme of what is important is thus to ask questions about the torment and to be aware of any metaphorical replies. Another way is to ask about areas of the client's life in which problems have a less dominant function: What does (or did) the client do when he is (or was) more free? When does the client describe enjoying a satisfying or positive experience, no matter how limited or brief?

Returning to Andrew:

> *Therapist:*   I was thinking about what you said about belonging,
>   about singing in a choir, for example. I understand that
>   you generally miss that. But yet I also think that you

must have some kind of experience of being in a group, given that you find it enticing.

Andrew: That was ages ago.

Therapist: How long ago?

Andrew: Before it all went pear-shaped, before all the repulsive stuff. I remember when we played soccer...

Therapist: Soccer?

Andrew: When I was at school. I was on the school team.

Therapist: Tell me more!

Andrew: I was a midfielder. You know, you got the ball, you passed it. When it went well, when we scored and I helped set up the goal, the feeling of having scored or won a match—it was us together, as a team, you know?

Therapist: How did it feel to be part of the team?

Andrew: (*smiling slightly*) Wonderful.

Therapist: In the here and now, if you could join that choir would it be something like being 'together as a team'?

Andrew: If things went well, yeah. Though it feels pretty remote.

Therapist: Right. As if it were almost impossible. Would that be something we could work on together? That you take steps toward being one of the team, in some sense? That you do something that makes that more likely?

If the dialogue suggests that this metaphorical expression "to be one of the team" says something important, several follow-up questions present themselves:

"What 'team' is available to you right now? What could you do that would be a step in that direction? What role would you like on that team?"

Catching Your Own Metaphors

In the previous chapter, I described principles for how metaphors can be created by the therapist. But, as is the case for the client, most metaphors the therapist uses are spontaneous rather than consciously contrived. This is something that the therapist can be attentive to and make use of. If she observes what spontaneously appears in her own imagination during the dialogue, she will find many rich pickings. Naturally, what comes to her might mainly concern herself rather than her client; this also must be borne in mind when catching metaphors that are spontaneously uttered by the client—there is always a risk that the therapist will be too hasty to interpret the client's meaning on her own terms. The importance of examining what function a metaphor has for the client cannot be stressed enough. Metaphors that the therapist catches in herself always have a large margin of error, of course. At the same time, the client, during a therapeutic dialogue, is a vital part of the context with which the therapist interacts, and what then spontaneously surfaces can be assumed to connect with what the client says and otherwise does. Noting and making use of our own reactions in our interaction with clients is an important part of our therapeutic repertoire. Spontaneously surfacing metaphors are part of these potentially useful phenomena. But only potentially useful. Whether a specific, spontaneously surfacing metaphor that the therapist notes in herself is actually helpful to the dialogue or not can rarely be determined by an immediate theoretical analysis—the process is too rapid for such a deliberate intellectual assessment, and the therapist must try her way ahead.

One tool that the therapist can use when considering whether or not to use such a metaphor is, of course, the set of principles I mentioned before. As always: Does the therapist know what she wants to attempt? What is important to emphasize in the here and now? Does this metaphor fit into the strategy that the therapist now wishes to apply? If so, she can try it. Since we can only guess what is useful and seldom know for sure, we must express ourselves candidly so that the client is able to dismiss what he considers unhelpful. On the other hand, deciding not to try a metaphor out of uncertainty can deprive us of a valuable therapeutic tool. In this context, I invite you to recall the research into psychotherapeutic metaphor use that I described in chapter 5, which demonstrated that a determiner of a metaphor's effectiveness is how much the therapist and client are able to cooperate on its use. If the therapist introduces a metaphor into the dialogue, it is therefore more important for her to keep an eye on how her client interacts with it than to concentrate on whether she herself deems it "theoretically correct." In other words: is this a metaphor that will inspire cooperation? Will the client use it, or part of it, in the ensuing dialogue? If he does, the metaphor is probably helpful; if not, the therapist would be wise to abandon it, no matter how theoretically correct it might seem.

This brings us to the theme of the next chapter: creating metaphors together.

CHAPTER 12

Cocreating Metaphors

In my previous account of how metaphors can be used in psychotherapy, I have—for pedagogical reasons—drawn a distinction between those generated by the therapist on the one hand and by the client on the other. In both cases, however, it is clear in most of my examples that a metaphor that proves clinically valuable is usually developed by both parties in dialogue with each other. A "ready" metaphor initiated in its entirety by the therapist, such as the bus metaphor used in ACT (see chapter 9), can also often be developed or nuanced by the client, at least if he takes it to be meaningful or pertinent. The client latches on to a certain part of the metaphor and compares it with something new or adjusts it. In the bus example, he might say, "My bus is overcrowded—it's total chaos in there!" When the therapist captures a metaphor that the client has just used, her job in this respect is to ask questions so that the metaphor can be developed to clarify some important aspect of the therapeutic work.

In the admittedly rather limited research on the kind of metaphor use that correlates with favorable therapy outcomes, the degree of cooperation on metaphor creation seems to be a key factor (see chapter 5). Successful therapies often appear to be characterized by the recurrence of certain critical metaphors that are used and/or developed by both dialogical parties. Although this has, up to a point, also been clearly seen in my earlier examples, I want to concentrate in this chapter on "cocreation" and how it can be facilitated by the therapist.

I will continue to use as a guide the three principles of therapeutic work I presented earlier. Again, the therapist is not to initiate any metaphor development, but focus on the ones which can be assumed to serve these three principles.

When a given metaphor takes up more space in the dialogue and is developed jointly by the therapist and the client, usually not just one of the three principles will be applied. Rather, the therapist will traverse all three, moving from one to the other as circumstances dictate. And as I commented earlier, the three principles overlap to a degree. Doing a functional analysis is the basic task of the therapist. And if the conversation turns to events in the client's experience and to what he does in these situations, the chances are that metaphorical expressions used will be useful for at least one part of the A-B-C sequence. It is then up to the therapist to use the metaphor to help the client establish an observational distance from the relevant reactions he has (those that are antecedent to his problematic behavior), and to identify what is important to the client and what he can do to behaviorally orient himself toward it.

I will therefore now not address one principle at a time, but instead illustrate the process through a dialogue with one client at a time, showing how metaphors can be "cocreated" while the therapist roams across the three principles.

Cocreation with Catherine

Let us return, then, to the dialogue with Catherine and her account of how she feels at work. As we saw earlier (chapter 8), the therapist refrained from developing a spontaneous metaphorical expression that Catherine used, namely that "it just kind of overflowed." Let us see now how an alternative response intended to develop this metaphor might look:

> *Therapist:*   When did it start?
>
> *Catherine:*   Just after the morning coffee break. I got a lot of urgent emails and then Petra came by with material that had to be looked at before the meeting we're having on Friday. It all just kind of overflowed.
>
> *Therapist:*   Where? Where did it overflow?
>
> *Catherine:*   (*frowning a little*) Where? In me, I suppose…?
>
> *Therapist:*   Where in you?
>
> *Catherine:*   Everywhere. It just overflows into me.

Therapist:	Everywhere… Quite a lot, in other words. But where would you say most obviously?
Catherine:	Here in my throat, I guess. *(Touches her throat with her right hand.)* And in my head *(moving her hand to her head)*.
Therapist:	Okay, mostly there. Are there places in your body where you can't notice it overflowing?
Catherine:	Not sure. Maybe…
Therapist:	How about your toes? Do you notice it there?
Catherine:	*(smiling slightly)* No, not in my toes.
Therapist:	Mostly in the throat and head… How about your stomach?
Catherine:	I feel it there too, but it's mostly up here. *(Touches her throat again.)*
Therapist:	And not in your toes. You don't feel anything in your toes.

Let us return once more to the three change principles that are to guide our work with metaphors (chapter 7). How are they used in the above dialogue with Catherine?

- **Functional analysis:** When Catherine first says that "it just kind of overflowed," the therapist takes the metaphor as a description of a relevant part of the antecedent functions for problematic behavior; that is to say that under the circumstances of experiencing this (A), Catherine does things (B) that do not work well (C). In the questions that follow, the therapist tries to help Catherine notice these functions and assumes that the metaphor's source (water overflowing) says something about how she feels in this situation (the metaphor's target) and that her being more aware of this will benefit her.

- **Establishing an observational distance:** When Catherine says that this experience is "everywhere" the therapist validates parts of this (that it is "quite a lot") but tries through her follow-up questions to help Catherine be more exact in her observation. This leads to the question about whether she feels this as much in her toes. Her discomfort might well have been felt there, but the therapist guesses that this is not the case, as Catherine then confirms. The hope is that this closer attention and distinguishing between sensations in different body parts will make it more likely that Catherine establishes an observational distance from her intimidating experience. Here, then, the therapist switches to the second of the three principles. This could be accomplished further with questions such as, "Who notices how it overflows in your throat?" and, "Who notices how it feels in your toes?" All this is done so that Catherine's torment will change functionally, and no longer contribute to her defective strategy.

- **Clarifying what is important in life and what concrete steps can be taken in that direction:** This third principle is not brought to the fore in the above dialogue.

Metaphors also originally introduced by the therapist can similarly be developed with the client. Take the metaphor that described Catherine's strategy as "trying to shift a rock with a lever" (chapter 8).

Therapist: And I wonder: isn't this a bit what it's like at work? You try to get everything done, to take responsibility for sorting everything out. In a variety of ways, as you've described. Every day, the same struggle. And I wonder: do you ever shift that rock?

Catherine: No, I don't. But it's as if I know of no other way. It's what I've always done. If I give it my all, I can do it.

Therapist: And now you're giving it your all. But the rock won't budge.

Catherine: Maybe I'm not giving it my all, then.

Therapist: Okay. So what you have to do is give it more. Get a better grip on the lever and thrust it in deeper. Have you tried that before?

Catherine: The whole time. It doesn't work. It just tires me out.

Therapist: So there's a consequence. You give it everything and just get more and more tired. And the rock's still there. And here's another thing: what if there are other rocks you can move, maybe ones that would be important to you but that you're overlooking because you've told yourself you have to move this one first. The other ones are just lying there waiting, but you never get around to them.

Catherine: I don't know. It hasn't really crossed my mind. I've just got to do this, move this rock. It's sitting there, right in front of me. But now that you mention it, I do miss quite a lot. There's a lot I can't handle.

Therapist: What if you were free to use your lever, your ability, exactly how you wanted to. If you were able to choose your rocks, so to speak. Which rocks are important to you, would you say?

Again: What is the therapist trying to do in terms of the three principles?

- **Functional analysis:** The therapist starts with the main point of the metaphor introduced: the part of the functional analysis intended to clarify the connection between what Catherine does and the consequences of this—between B and C.

- **Establishing an observational distance:** The simple fact that the connection is talked about in the form of a metaphor can help to establish a certain observational distance for Catherine, even if it is not as much in focus as in the "overflowing" example.

- **Clarifying what is important in life and what concrete steps can be taken in that direction:** The therapist notes that Catherine is running with the introduced metaphor and develops it by asking questions intended to increase the likelihood that Catherine connects with things that are important to her and that would motivate change: "If you could choose which rocks ..."

The following is another example of how the therapist develops a given metaphor, in this case introduced by Catherine.

Therapist: When you find it "overflowing," what do you do? How do you relate to the situation?

Catherine: I try to stop it—shut if off, I guess you could say. Like I try to find the tap and turn it off. But it just doesn't work and I just end up floating away in the current.

Therapist: Where do you float away to?

Catherine: Away to everything that has to get done. To all the musts.

Therapist: If you found that you could actually start swimming, could choose the direction to swim in, where would you swim to?

What is the therapist trying to do here in terms of the three principles?

- **Functional analysis:** In the first question, the therapist establishes the circumstance (the experience of it overflowing, A) that seems relevant and directs her question to what Catherine then does (B). Catherine replies within the bounds of the metaphor. The therapist's next question is directed at the consequence of Catherine's action, C. Again, Catherine answers within the metaphor. The entire sequence is thus an example of a shared functional analysis, performed within the framework of a metaphor introduced by the client but developed jointly.

- **Establishing an observational distance:** Again, this principle is not in focus, but (again) the fact that both circumstance and action (trying to turn off the water, floating away) are mentioned metaphorically indicates a possible observational distance.

- **Clarifying what is important in life and what concrete steps can be taken in that direction:** Toward the end of the dialogue, after Catherine has understood something about what she does and where it leads, the therapist asks her about what direction she would like to take: "Where would you swim to?" She also intimates that such a strategy could be available to Catherine: "… if you found you could actually start swimming …"

Cocreation with Barry

In the earlier example with Barry, the dialogue centred mainly on his experience of despondency and what he does when he has that experience. Let us assume that in a conversation about what is important to him, he refers more to his pain and the impediment it constitutes for him.

Barry: But I'm never going to be able to join in in the way I want to. The pain is just too bad. I just can't do it.

Therapist: Where do you feel the pain the most?

Barry: In my neck and shoulders. It's heavy and kind of tight.

Therapist: This tightness, can you tell me more about what it's like?

Barry: Like having a vise over my neck. It's being turned and I'm stuck in it.

Therapist: If we say it's a real vise, what's it made of? Can you describe it?

Barry: Wooden, one of the old-fashioned kinds you used to get on carpenters' benches.

Therapist: Color?

Barry: Brown, wood-colored.

Therapist: Okay. Is the vise always as tight, or does it vary?

Barry: I feel it most of the time, but sometimes it's worse. When it gets really tight it's terrible. Almost as if I can't move. I can, of course, but it really hurts. I just want to give up.

Therapist: Is it tight in one place—sometimes more sometimes less—or is it tight in several places?

Barry:	(*silent, thinking*) It's in several places, over the neck and down the shoulders. Different at different times.
Therapist:	That vise that causes you so much pain. Does it have anything to tell you?
Barry:	How do you mean?
Therapist:	Would you say that when it tightens, the vise is telling you something?
Barry:	If it is, it's just to give up. There's no point, you know?
Therapist:	Do you do as it says, would you say?
Barry:	You mean give up? Not completely. But in many ways I suppose I do.
Therapist:	Like what you just said, that you'll never be able to join in, not in the way that you want to?
Barry:	Yes, that's what it's like when its most painful.
Therapist:	The brown vise tightens, tells you that there's no point and that you might as well give up. So you give up— some things, anyway. Perhaps even some important things?
Barry:	I guess so.
Therapist:	That brown vise, who is it who notices it?
Barry:	(*a bit baffled*) Me, I suppose…?
Therapist:	Right. And who notices that sometimes it's really tight and sometimes not?
Barry:	Me.
Therapist:	And as much as someone gives up, who is it that gives up?
Barry:	Me. Though I don't want to. I don't want to give up.

What is it that the therapist is trying to do in terms of the three principles?

- **Functional analysis:** Barry states a circumstance (A) in which he "just can't do it"—namely his pain. By directing questions at this phenomenon, the therapist helps him to explore this circumstance more closely. On one level, this is a nascent functional analysis. The therapist assumes that Barry, in the presence of his pain, does things that in the long run do him a disservice. By looking more closely at the details of how Barry experiences this, the therapist approaches a possible question about what Barry then does (B) in the presence of his pain and how this works out for him (C). But at the same time, she asks about the pain in a way that helps Barry use a metaphorical expression (the vise), and when it is delivered, asks follow-up questions that develop the metaphor.

- **Establishing an observational distance:** When the therapist deliberately asks probing questions about relevant antecedent functions (Barry's experience of pain) in this metaphorical, concrete manner, she does so to establish an observational distance. People's experience of vises, or of any objects that have a color or other physical property, is one of objects in our environment. When Barry's own responses (pain, for example) are talked about in this way (an external object, a vise, serves as the metaphor's source and Barry's experience of pain as its target), the likelihood increases that Barry will establish an observational distance from this experience of his and thus that the influence of this experience over his behavior will change. The therapist establishes, in the dialogue, a context that makes it more likely that Barry will frame his experience of pain (and what it is telling him) in hierarchy with the deictic I (to describe the process more technically through the vocabulary of RFT).

- **Clarifying what is important in life and what concrete steps can be taken in that direction:** While the therapist does not use this third principle explicitly in her conversation with Barry here, Barry's final comment that he does not want to give up offers the therapist an opportunity to do so by inviting questions about what it is that Barry does not want to give up and what would be an important direction to take even in the presence of the vise.

When Barry seems a little freer in relation to the experience that has so far had such a hold over him (the pain, the feeling of despondency), the therapist can try to introduce questions about how Barry can direct his steps toward what is important to him. Naturally, this can, like so much else in psychological therapy, be effected through literal language and not necessarily through the medium of metaphors. However, I shall stick to the theme of this book and present yet another example of how a codeveloped metaphor can be used.

The following dialogue takes place before a long-since planned family gathering that Barry has been looking forward to. The get-together will be at his brother's place, and some cousins he has not seen for a while will be there. They are similar in age and were close some years ago, and the cousins have written to express their excitement at seeing Barry again. All this has made his expressed wish to be "one of the gang" more immediate. It has also brought up his insecurities about meeting with his brother. So a few days before the gathering, his pain grows worse and he is thrown into doubt about what to do.

Barry:	It's like I'm stuck, somehow, like I can't move. It's that feeling of despondency again. It's enough to make me want to quit.
Therapist:	This feeling stuck, is it the vise again? Like it's sort of jammed?
Barry:	Yeah, it's like I have to get rid of it. Like it's just got to let go somehow.
Therapist:	And in your experience, does it? Does waiting for it to ease pay off?
Barry:	No, I've had the pain for so long, you know. It can ease up a bit sometimes, but then it gets really bad again.
Therapist:	So the brown vise tightens and then eases up sometimes. But then it tightens again and you feel like you're stuck.
Barry:	Exactly.

Therapist: Who decides here, the vise or you?

Barry: About the pain? Well, it ain't me, that's for sure!

Therapist: You don't control the vise, and it's not up to you how tight it feels. But imagine this: if you're going to this family gathering, you will have to take the vise with you. It's understandable that you want it to release its grip but your experience seems to tell you that you'll never know how tight it'll be. Sometimes it eases off, sometimes it tightens. What if you take the vise with you and go? For the sake of something that's important to you?

Barry: That's what I want, but it's so hard.

Therapist: If you were to take the vise with you, what is it that entices you to? What would you do it for?

Barry: To belong, to socialize, reminisce. About the fun we used to have.

Therapist: When we talk about it, can you picture it?

Barry: Yeah, I can. It's a long time ago but we did a bunch of fun stuff together. I think it'd be a real blast to see them again.

Therapist: *(noting that Barry is growing animated)* It looks like you're already feeling it.

Barry: I am. I'd love to see them again, if I could.

What is it the therapist is trying to do in terms of the three principles?

- **Functional analysis:** The circumstances (A) in which Barry tends to resume his problematic strategy (B) are once again brought to the fore. The therapist asks questions to clarify this very correlation and the usual consequences of Barry's behavior (C).

- **Establishing an observational distance:** By using the cocreated metaphorical expression (the brown vise), the therapist tries again to change the verbal context to increase the probability of Barry establishing an observational distance from his own experience (framing his own response in hierarchy with the deictic I) so that its influence on the rest of his behavior will be altered.

- **Clarifying what is important in life and what concrete steps can be taken in that direction:** When the therapist detects a little more flexibility in Barry in relation to the obstacles he experiences (pain, despondency), the therapist asks about a possible alternative (to take the vise with him) in order to reach what Barry himself articulates as important. When the therapist notes that Barry has contact with something that engages him, the focus shifts to this to enhance its motivational function.

When Barry feels less shackled by the impediments he experiences, the therapist can choose to focus further on an alternative, possibly more effective behavior:

Barry: Yeah, I'd love to see them again, if I could.

Therapist: So I ask again: Is it you or the vise that decides?

Barry: If I go? Me.

Therapist: As you said before, you seem unable to decide just how tight the vise sits. But I assume that if you were to take the vise with you and go it would have no choice in the matter. I mean, it can't move of its own accord, right?

Barry: No, of course not. It'd be hard, though. It'd be painful, and then I've got all these questions running around in my head. What are they going to say? What if I can't handle it? And what'll I say to my brother?

Therapist: Your head gives you a lot of questions. Are they new ones, or do you recognize them from before?

Barry: (*smiling slightly*) They're the same old ones.

Therapist: Have you got any good answers?

Barry: Nope.

> *Therapist:* I look at it like this: Sometimes our head isn't our friend. It goes on and on in the same old way and it's not very useful, not at the time. Sometimes all you've got to rely on is your feet. It's where you place your foot that you leave a footprint. And I'm wondering if that's not where you're at. How would it be to rely on your feet and turn them in the direction you want your footprints to follow?

By continuing to talk of Barry's pain in terms of a vise and to ask questions that distinguish between Barry as agent and the vise, the therapist strives to increase Barry's observational distance, in relation to his pain. She also persists in presenting an alternative behavioral strategy by reference to the same metaphor (taking the vise with him), adding emphasis by shifting metaphor and suggesting he "rely on his feet": a new source for the same target, as described in chapter 8. Here too, Barry is encouraged to pay regard on the one hand to the unnerving questions that arise (his head talking), and on the other to his instruments of agency (him controlling where he puts his feet).

Cocreation with Andrew

We now return to the dialogue with Andrew as he describes himself as feeling like a tiny ant in social situations.

> *Therapist:* What's it like, when you turn into an ant?
>
> *Andrew:* I just get smaller. It's almost as if I don't exist. I don't belong. Want to get away. I'm a total failure. No one wants me there anyway.
>
> *Therapist:* It sounds pretty distressing.
>
> *Andrew:* (*sighs*) Empty, meaningless. It's at times like that I want to end it all. I might as well just disappear for real.
>
> *Therapist:* At times like that, when everything feels empty and meaningless, what do you tend to do?
>
> *Andrew:* Nothing. There's no point.

Therapist: Okay. So it's just empty and meaningless. At the same time here's what I think: we're always doing something. I mean, even when we abstain from doing things and do "nothing," even that is doing "something." Do you see what I mean?

Andrew: I guess you could say that. I go quiet, for example. Look away, almost as if I'm trying to make myself smaller somehow.

Therapist: In order that...?

Andrew: In order that no one'll see me, that I can escape.

Therapist: Would you say that when you feel like an ant, you easily 'ant' yourself?

Andrew: *(smiling slightly)* You could put it like that. I don't want to be an ant, but I still try to make myself tiny, so yeah, you could say I ant myself.

Therapist: If you could stop yourself anting, if you could choose to be another animal in these situations, what animal would you be?

Andrew: A dog!

Therapist: A dog. What kind of dog is that?

Andrew: You know, a dog doesn't turn away. It goes up to you, wagging its tail, expects to be included. It doesn't have to be in the center of things. It just wants to join in.

Therapist: Okay. And there's a difference between "'anting" and "dogging." The dog walks up to people, expecting to be "included." What would it look like, in that kind of situation, if you would do some "dogging"?

Andrew: *(silent at first)* It'd be horrible. And fantastic! If only I could...

> *Therapist:* Let's say you had one of those pills we talked about (*see the earlier dialogue with Andrew, chapter 10*), how do you think you'd do it? What would it be to "dog" in a situation like that?
>
> *Andrew:* I'd dare to go up to people, perhaps say something. Look them in the eye.

What is it the therapist trying to do in terms of the three principles?

- **Functional analysis:** The therapist captures a metaphor that Andrew has used and asks him to develop it. By, in turn, developing it with the help of a made-up verb (to "ant"), the therapist places the focus on what Andrew does (B) under the distressing circumstances he describes (A). Parts of a functional analysis, therefore, framed within a metaphor of feeling and acting as an ant.

- **Establishing an observational distance:** Talking of spontaneously aroused emotions and thoughts and Andrew's way of acting in the frame of this metaphor is intended to train him in this very aspect.

- **Clarifying what is important in life and what concrete steps can be taken in that direction:** By asking what animal Andrew would prefer to be, the metaphor is further developed and the focus shifted onto what Andrew could do to increase the chances of effecting the change he wants. The concrete follow-up questions are designed to help Andrew connect more with this possibility.

If a metaphor has been well-established in the dialogue, it is often an easy matter to recycle it:

> *Andrew:* I get that I have to change my behavior and not just cower away. I want to approach other people. But I find it so hard. Like yesterday. After the cinema when the people beside me started chatting. I could feel the knot tightening, and I knew just what would happen.
>
> *Therapist:* This reminds me of that book (*see the earlier dialogue with Andrew, chapter 9*). *The Repulsive Failure.* Did any

particular chapter come to mind yesterday when you were at the cinema?

Andrew: The last time I was at the cinema, a month or so ago—boy, how alienated did I feel afterward! Then there was old stuff, stuff with the neighbor from ages ago. I don't really know why it came up just then, but it's there a hell of a lot of the time.

Therapist: The same book, different chapters. Some chapters are tougher than others. What do you do when the book makes its presence known?

Andrew: The usual. Just go silent and look away. Run away.

Therapist: So that…?

Andrew: So that no one will see me, because I can't cope. It's hopeless, the same thing every time. And then I just dwell on it on the way home.

Therapist: Would I be right I saying that at first, when the book shows up, you act according to what it says? As if you're in the book and following it, as if it's a script for how you're to act. And then you stop and read some old chapters. Is that right?

Andrew: Yeah, that's right. Again and again. How do I get myself out of this?

Therapist: This is what I think: In situations like that, what steps would be steps outside of the book? Steps that are about something else. If you could take steps independent of this book, what kind of steps would those be, steps that would write a different story? What do you think?

What is it the therapist is trying to do in terms of the three principles?

- **Functional analysis:** A functional analysis is performed in the metaphorical frame of Andrew's troubling memories, thoughts, and feelings as a book. Under circumstances in which typical emotions and memories come to the fore (A), Andrew does certain things (B) and notices that what he does does not take him to where he wants to go (C).

- **Establishing an observational distance:** The main point of talking about this typical experience that Andrew has using the metaphor of a book is to develop his ability to adopt an observational distance, to establish "space" between Andrew as agent and the reactions he notices within himself.

- **Clarifying what is important in life and what concrete steps can be taken in that direction:** The metaphor is further developed to indicate a possible alternative, and the therapist asks questions to help Andrew approach it.

CHAPTER 13

Metaphors and Experiential Exercises

In experiential exercises, the therapist suggests and carries out different types of concrete activities with the client that are hopefully beneficial to the therapeutic process. This approach is pivotal to ACT (Hayes, Strosahl, & Wilson, 2012) and has a long history in psychological therapy. Classic exercises of this kind are the "empty chair" and the "two-chairs exercise" used by Gestalt therapy (Greenberg, Rice, & Elliot, 1993), sculpture exercises in family therapy (Hearn & Lawrence, 1981), and psychodrama activities (Karp & Holmes, 1998). What CBT practitioners refer to as "behavioral experiments" (Bennet-Levi, Butler, Fennel, Hackman, Mueller et al., 2004) share many points of contact with this approach, and there is also a striking similarity with different types of exposure interventions in the presence of the therapist in classic behavioral therapy (Lang & Helbig-Lang, 2012).

What I will now describe thus overlaps with interventions found in different schools of psychological therapy. At the same time, it would be a gross simplification to say that "it's all the same." Even interventions that might look similar can be used in different ways and with different intentions, often in combination with one or another theoretical model. So let me begin by describing experiential exercises from a behavior analytic perspective (see chapter 3), in accordance with the rest of this book.

In behavior analysis, the subject of our analysis is the interaction between a given behavior and the context in which it is performed. The point is that the analysis done should help us influence said behavior, provided that this is a change the client wants. The therapist is best positioned to contribute to change when, of course, the problematic behavior is acted out in her presence on what I have referred to as the "first scene" (Ramnerö & Törneke, 2008; Törneke, 2010). This is because the therapist is part of the regnant context of the behavior and thus has immediate access to at least some of the influencing factors. At the same time, it is in the client's life outside the therapy room—the "second scene"—that he desires change.

As has been described earlier in this book, it is not uncommon for the client's problem behavior to occur in interaction with the therapist, so it is important that she be aware of this and seize upon the opportunity to intervene for a change of what happens in the "here and now." (Compare with the concept of "working within the framework of the transference" in psychodynamic therapy.) The point of experiential exercises is, however, for the therapist not only to seize upon what emerges but also to actively initiate relevant behavioral sequences in agreement with the client. In principle, this is the same procedure as in exposure treatment that has long been used as part of behavior therapy. Take the treatment for spider phobia. The therapist does not just make do with talking about how the client is to relate to spiders but actually seeks out or stages the relevant situation using a real spider to work on the client's way of acting while present and best placed to do so. Effectively the same strategy applies when working with OCD—the therapist seeks out a situation in which the client's problem manifests itself—and with PTSD, where the therapist does not primarily look for extraneous triggers of the client's problem but does things in consultation with him that arouse relevant memories. Together they then work on the client's interaction with these memories as they are present.

Exposure does not necessarily require the therapist's presence. For all problems where exposure is usually applied, the therapist advises the client on, for instance, how he is to relate to spiders, circumstances that normally evoke compulsive actions or elicit traumatic memories. Sometimes this is all it takes and the client can then expose himself to the relevant factors by himself and in that way bring about change. This is an important part of the home assignments in CBT. But everyone who has experience with this type of treatment knows that sound advice does not always help, and if the therapist can initiate relevant situations with the client when she is present it will open up other opportunities for influence that are of benefit to the client. This is at the very heart of why experiential exercises are used. The intention is to stage a relevant situation and help the client discern his own strategy to address his problem and to identify and practice alternative strategies.

Experiential Exercises as Metaphors

So what connects all this about experiential exercises and the theme of this book, namely the use of metaphors in psychotherapy? Let me return once again to classic exposure interventions to make a comparison. In exposure for spider phobia, the therapist uses actual spiders on the assumption that it will establish a situation in the here and now (the first scene) that is sufficiently analogous to the situation in the client's own life (the second scene) in which he experiences his problems. The same applies when the therapist and the client seek out a situation that can be assumed to increase the risk of compulsive behavior or when the therapist asks the client with PTSD, as part of the exposure process, to recall distressing memories. The assumption is that this establishes a situation that is congruous with the problem context and if the client can be made to adopt a different strategy in these situations than he normally would, he is more likely to learn something new and thereby to change. Clearly, if we think about it, we can only establish a situation that is *similar*; after all, no one situation is identical to another. And besides, there is one element to the initiated situation that sets it apart from the typical in the client's life: the presence of the therapist. The actual strategy used in exposure therapy assumes, however, that the situations initiated in this "artificial" manner are sufficiently like the actual problem contexts to be opportunities for readjusting experiences and thus for change.

Experiential exercises take the principle of "sufficiently similar, initiated situations" one step further than classic exposure therapy. For someone who interacts with metaphors there are many ways in which things can be similar, as we have seen. One thing can stand for another. This implies that something that is done in the form of an exercise with the therapist and that in many respects is different from the client's everyday problem situation can still serve as an analogy or a metaphor and thus affect the client's problem at the crucial time. Let me illustrate this with a typical experiential exercise taken from ACT called the "life line" (Dahl, Plumb, Stewart, & Lundgren, 2009).

This exercise can be done in different ways, but the main thrust of it is this: the therapist asks the client to stand up and arranges an open space where he can move backward and forward. She uses something the client has previously declared as important and points in a particular direction with reference to the open space, saying something like, "Let's say that where you're standing is *now* in your life and that walking in that direction would be in accordance with whom you would like to be (as a parent, employee, friend, or whatever)." The therapist then asks the client to take steps in that direction and thus to "move toward what I want." As he advances, the therapist can interpose the psychological obstacles that the client has described from his life, such as adverse symptoms (anxiety, fatigue, hopelessness, distressing memories, and so on), by physically blocking his way and saying things that are typical of the perceived obstacles, or by holding up notes bearing descriptions of them based on the earlier dialogue.

The therapist then stages how the client usually acts in these situations as a deviation from the line toward where he wants to go in order to circumvent the obstacle, for example, or obey its implicit orders. If, for instance, a typical obstacle is anxiety and thoughts of going mad, the therapist holds up a note with the words "Anxiety, I'm going mad" and asks, "What do you normally do in situations like this?" When the client has replied ("I turn away" or "I try to understand why it gets like this," for example) the therapist tries to make the client decide if this behavior takes him forward on the line or if it is in fact a departure from the line. If the latter is the case, the therapist asks the client to illustrate this by stopping or stepping off the line. In this way it is possible, within the bounds of the exercise, to go to different situations, illustrate different behaviors, and ask questions about their consequences and whether these actions lead forward on the life line toward what the client wants or whether they are examples of vicious circles.

One aim of this approach is to help the client recognize overarching behavioral strategies and identify detrimental ones as "departures from the direction I want to take." Similarly, the exercise provides a context in which the client can recognize and practice more effective strategies. If the therapist assumes that a common problematic strategy is to give up overall life values in fruitless attempts to control or eliminate spontaneously aroused responses such as distressing thoughts and emotions (experiential avoidance), she can illustrate a more accepting strategy by writing the obstacles on Post-it notes and asking the client, instead of deviating from the line when they appear, to attach them to his clothes and continue on his way. The line can also be used to return to events that occurred long ago in the client's life, perhaps to those that are of probable significance to how his current strategies were first established or are otherwise seen by him as illustrative. Here as well the line is used to pinpoint the obstacles that arose in these situations and clarify how the client responded to them: "How did that work out for you?" "Maybe the strategy worked then, but does it now?" "Maybe the strategy caused problems for you already then?"— all illustrated with forward movement on the line or stopping or stepping off it in the presence of experiential obstacles.

If the above exercise is to work metaphorically and be of help to the client, the same conditions are required as with other kinds of metaphor use. The point of the exercise is for it to serve as a source and the client's life experience (the second scene) to serve as the target. As described earlier (figure 8.2, chapter 8) three things must be in place. First: *The metaphor's target must be a phenomenon that is functionally important for this individual client.*

The exercise described above is intended to stage the client's behavior in situations in which psychological phenomena present obstacles. This must therefore be relevant. The client's own behavior must be part of the problem, which in terms of this book's premises is a prerequisite of all psychotherapy. We can thus assume that the metaphor's target is relevant if we judge the client to have a chance to benefit from psychotherapy. The second condition is: *The metaphor's source must correspond to central parts of its target.*

This can simply be expressed thus: the source of the metaphor must be such that the client recognizes in the metaphor his own experience. An experiential exercise must therefore be designed so that the client can relate personally to it and feel that what he does in it is "like how it is for me." It is therefore absolutely essential to check with the client that this is the case. The third condition is: *The metaphor's source must embody a property or function that is more salient there than it is in its target.*

That this characterizes an effective metaphor is a decisive reason for using experiential exercises in the first place. The therapist seeks a concrete source that can be useful for clarifying both the client's problematic and possible alternative behavioral strategies. If the exercises used comprise discrete and distinct actions they will, provided that the second condition is fulfilled, become metaphorical sources with properties that are more salient than the processes in the client's life constituting the metaphor's target. Physically walking a few feet in a room, stopping when bits of paper are held up and either stepping aside or continuing, is presumably clearer than the more complex sequences the client goes through in his real life that are at the center of the therapeutic process. The crucial question is whether these simple actions are actually similar to those that are the intended target of the metaphorical exercise. In other words, can the client relate to the exercise? If not, the exercise will not work metaphorically.

Why Experiential Metaphors?

My point so far is that experiential exercises can be used in psychotherapy as metaphors. So what distinguishes these metaphors from metaphors in general, and why should they be assumed to be particularly beneficial? The answer to this question is in the description of how metaphors work that makes up the theoretical foundation of this entire book. Metaphors are often such that very basic and concrete human experiences make up their sources (see chapter 1). In virtually all languages, the human experience of moving through space seems to provide the source for metaphors of time as something with a spatial dimension: the future is "ahead" of us and the past "behind." The conceptual metaphor "more is up" is also rooted in the universal human experience that "if I get more of something physical, the pile (or level) gets higher." Metaphors often use concrete, distinct phenomena as a source of utterances about more abstract or nebulous target phenomena. In this respect, doing experiential exercises is nothing "special," but simply a typical way of creating effective metaphors.

Let us draw comparisons with some of the clinical metaphors described earlier. ACT uses the metaphor of "digging in a hole" to describe a fruitless behavioral strategy (see chapter 8). Another metaphor for the same phenomenon as used in the dialogue with Catherine (chapter 8) was "trying to shift a large rock with a lever." Let us assume that Catherine has no experience of digging herself deeper into a hole but knows just what it is like to try to shift a rock. The latter metaphor then has a source that for her is more experiential and concrete than the former. Does this make the latter metaphor better or more effective for change work? There is some preliminary experimental work that supports the position that this would make a metaphor more effective (Riuz & Luciano, 2015; Sierra et al., 2016), and theoretically there are also reasons to believe so, given the general function of metaphor.

What distinguishes metaphors that use experiential exercises as a source is that the source is created in dialogue with the therapist, in the client's experience of the exercise. "Imagine if what you experience in life is like in this exercise." If the exercise includes physical movement (along the life line, say), this can in itself be essential and can increase the chances that the client will, at critical moments, remember key events and therefore have a marker for "what he must and mustn't do." Patterns of motion might also have other non-verbal functions of importance to change. We learn not only through linguistic, cognitive processes but also through what behavior analysts refer to as "direct contingencies." And although this fundamental learning pathway quickly becomes verbal at every moment (it acquires "meaning") via the process described in the section on RFT (chapter 4) this does not diminish the significance of direct, nonverbal, or nonsymbolic learning (Hayes, 1997). Here, experiential exercises tie in with therapeutic models that stress sensorimotor components in therapeutic work (Ogden & Fisher, 2015; Ogden, Pain, & Fisher, 2006; Porges, 2011).

In sum, experiential exercises are quite simply a means of therapeutically creating a functional metaphorical language by setting up experiences in the moment that can serve as a source for targeting important phenomena in the client's life outside the therapeutic context.

Experiential Exercises and the Three Therapeutic Strategies

How do these exercises then relate to the three guiding principles of therapy? Let us take the life line as an example.

What is it that the therapist is trying to do in terms of the three principles?

- **Functional analysis:** This is the very heart of the exercise. What the client does (B) in different typical situations is illustrated, including both the problematic strategy (stopping, stepping aside) and the alternative strategy (moving ahead). The circumstance under which the client does this (A) is illustrated by the therapist's imposition of obstacles represented as written notes. What follows (C) is also part of the exercise in the experience of establishing vicious circles or of acting in the direction to what you want.

- **Establishing an observational distance:** The client's interaction with his own behavior and the obstacles he experiences as concrete, observable phenomena (walking on a line, the notes) is intended to increase the likelihood of this happening.

- **Clarifying what is important in life and what concrete steps can be taken in that direction:** The experience of walking in the direction toward what he wants (to follow the line, even in the presence of what usually obstructs him) is intended to serve as a metaphorical source for how the client is to act to increase the chances of effecting change (the metaphor's target).

The life line is an exercise that clearly embraces all three therapeutic principles. But other exercises might differ in this respect and, like metaphors in general, more explicitly concentrate on only one of the principles. Let us return to our three clients to see what different exercises can look like and how they can be used.

Experiential Exercise with Catherine

Catherine has described her stress, how she gets hot and how her heart starts to pound, and her feelings of being overwhelmed and of having to make more of an effort just to keep up. One aspect of what she tries to do in these situations is to rid herself of this experience—or, as she puts it metaphorically, to turn the tap off to stop it all overflowing. The therapist recognizes this as experiential avoidance and feels that Catherine would need to pay closer attention to what she does and what this leads to, and to adopt an observational distance from the reactions that she tries to "turn off." The following would be a possible exercise:

Therapist: I have an exercise that I sometimes like to use. Would you like to give it a go?

Catherine: Sure!

Therapist: (*picking up a notepad*) I'm going to write down some of the things that come into your head in these situations, the things that plague you and that you feel you want to turn off. Your pounding heart, for instance (*writing it down*). What else?

Catherine: That I get so hot, that feeling of stress. That everything's just overflowing.

Therapist: (*writing down Catherine's words*) What about having to get everything done?

Catherine: That's like the conclusion, what everything leads up to.

Therapist: (*noting again what she has written and holding the notepad out to Catherine*) Hold your hand against this, against the pad and what's written on it.

Catherine: (*holding her palm up to the paper a little sheepishly*) Okay...

Therapist: (*pressing from her side*) Resist it! Keep it away from you!

Catherine: (*pressing with greater force*) Like this?

The therapist and Catherine both apply pressure to their respective sides of the notepad, which hovers back and forth in the space between them.

Therapist: Good. Take note of what this is like! (*Lowers the pad.*) Remember what that was like and compare it with this (*placing the pad in Catherine's lap text side up so that she can still read it*).

Catherine: (*first quietly, looking down at the words*) Yeah, that certainly was different.

Therapist: In what way?

Catherine: It was easier having it in my lap, of course. In a sense. Though it made me feel uncomfortable, too. I don't like that sort of thing.

Therapist: Maybe you can say the two positions are the same and yet different. The same because in both you have contact with the paper and what's written on it.

Catherine: Okay, although resisting it like I did takes more energy. But then it also feels good in a way, too. At least I'm doing something.

Therapist: If you were to compare how much of everything else that's going on in here that you notice when you resist the pad or have it in your lap, is it the same or is it different?

Catherine: Resisting it demands all my attention and my mind's totally set on keeping it away from me. At first when I get it in my lap and see what's written on it it's the same, but then it changes. It just sits there, you know, and I can let other things in.

Therapist: Okay. If we say, within the scope of the exercise, that you'd like to do something different, like leave, borrow my phone on the desk there to call someone, or look out the window (*Catherine has to stand up and walk a few steps to do this*), in which of these positions are you more free to do it?

Catherine: When it's in my lap. In the other position I'm totally taken up with keeping the pad away from me.

Therapist: Taken up with keeping it away from you... And having it in your lap, how was that?

Catherine: It was uncomfortable, at least at first. I can see clearly what's written there and it just reminds me of all the stuff I can't handle. It's weird, but it was also kind of liberating, seeing it so like that in black and white... I guess that's when other things start to come in.

Therapist: Which of the positions is most like what you do out in life, like in your job, do you think?

Here, the therapist asks a question that, implicitly, is a decisive test of whether this exercise will be of any benefit to Catherine. It is the second item of the three that must be fulfilled for a metaphor to work (the metaphor's source must correspond to central parts of its target—see figure 8.2, chapter 8). In this case, the metaphor's target is things that Catherine does in life in response to her experience of stress and the different forms of discomfort she describes—above all her efforts to keep this experience away from her, to turn it off. The source is the different aspects of the exercise. And now the all important question: does this metaphor work for Catherine? Or: can she relate to the exercise?

Catherine: Resisting. It's what I do all the time. It's so obvious to me. That's exactly it. The whole time, actually.

The dialogue during and after such an exercise can take very different forms. Some clients throw the pad onto the floor as soon as it is placed in their lap. The therapist should be open to the client's experience and use it continuously as her point of reference. The point of the exercise is not persuasion; it is exploration. It is a means of trying to stage behavior that is clinically relevant and help the client observe it. Let us assume that Catherine had actually reacted in this way, and flung the notepad away from her as soon as it landed in her lap. What could the therapist have done? Perhaps state what Catherine did and ask her what she thought about the situation. An option would be to then suggest that throwing the notepad onto the floor is a variant of the first position, to keep the difficult experience away from her. And that clearly this strategy is altogether natural for her.

There are many possible things to glean from the above exercise. What are the pros and cons of the different behaviors? In which of the two positions is the client more free to act in the desired manner in life? If Catherine is fully cognizant that what she does is to "resist" her problems, what would it then mean to have them "in her lap" and to do so in her normal daily life? A possible continuation is to use the exercise as a metaphor or analogue for something that can be done as a home assignment.

Therapist: I've got a suggestion for something you can do until our next appointment. I wonder if you can just take note of when you resist, just a couple of times if and when it happens. Can you do that?

Catherine: Of course. And stop resisting?

Therapist: I wouldn't worry about that just now. Resist or ignore. What I want you to do is to take note of when you find yourself in that position.

Another focus in a post-exercise home assignment could be:

Therapist: If "having it in your lap" could give you greater latitude to act in different situations and if you could, for some reason, suddenly do it at least once this coming week, in what situation would you most want this to happen?

Catherine: (*momentarily silent*) At the Friday meeting before lunch. That's when things get really bad and I really have to struggle.

Therapist: Shall we look a little more closely at the situation and see what you can do to have it more "in your lap"?

If the therapist wants to, she can at this stage delve into what is important for the client by not just asking for a concrete example in the coming week but also expanding the dialogue with questions about what would ultimately be gained from being able to have things in her lap. What areas could be changed and what would this look like in Catherine's mind?

An exercise like this not only can have a metaphorical function when performed, but it can also, if illustrating some essential phenomenon, accompany the therapy just like any other regular metaphor. In a situation in which Catherine returns with an account of a clinically relevant situation, the therapist can say things that refer back to an experiential exercise, as with the following questions:

"Would you say that that was pushing it away or having it in your lap?"

"If you want to have that in your lap, how would you go about doing it?"

"That sounds to me like an example of you having it more in your lap. Would you agree?"

What is it that the therapist is trying to do in terms of the three principles?

- **Functional analysis:** This is once again at the heart of the exercise. Simple movements in the therapy room are intended to illustrate both the problematic strategy (resisting) and a possible alternative strategy (having her aversive reactions in her lap). Questions are asked to clarify the consequences of each strategy.

- **Establishing an observational distance:** Turning the difficult experiences and symptoms the client describes into ink on paper and into something that has different effects on the client's behavior is an attempt to help her establish an observational distance from these phenomena.

- **Clarifying what is important in life and what concrete steps can be taken in that direction:** While this is not part of the exercise per se, it is included in the ensuing dialogue.

Experiential Exercises with Andrew

Andrew is very much identified with a story of himself, the book "The Repulsive Failure." In technical (RFT) terms, one could say that he acts in coordination with this narrative, making an important part of his therapy what I have referred to as the second therapeutic principle—namely, to train his ability to frame this narrative in a hierarchy with the deictic I: to establish an observational distance from the "book" in order to diminish its influence on his further behavior. The following is an experiential exercise intended to specifically train him in this ability, described here in a way that can be applied to effectively any client.

Therapist:	I have an exercise that you might benefit from. Would you like to give it a go?
Andrew:	Sure.
Therapist:	Then first I'd like you to look out the window.
Andrew:	*(turning around to face the window, which is behind him)* Okay...?

Therapist: I'd like you to look for something small and distinct that you can see. Maybe a tree branch or the corner of a roof. Whatever. Take something small but that you can still see. You don't have to tell me what it is; just focus your attention *there* (*a moment's silence*) on the thing you've chosen to concentrate on. If something else turns up, that is okay. Just notice that and turn your attention back to the thing you have chosen. (*Silence.*)

While you keep your focus there, I'd like you to notice a few things: notice that what you're looking at is *there* and that you, the observer, are *here.* The object I'm noticing *there*, me noticing it *here.* Note the distance or the space between you and the thing you're observing. (*Another moment of silence.*)

Now I'll ask you to leave what you see out there and look at something closer to you, maybe something in this room. Look around and choose something small again, some detail that's little but still visible. (*Pauses.*)

And again, I'll ask you to notice that, *there.* The observed object *there.* I, the one observing, *here.* Note again the distance, the space between you and it. (*Pauses.*)

From now on it might be easier if you shut your eyes, but you don't have to. Most people find it easier to do so, but it's up to you. Because now I'm going to ask you to observe something you can see in your mind's eye rather that with your real eyes. See if you can observe something you feel in your left foot when sitting there like you are now. Maybe the shoe pressing on a certain part or its sole having slightly more contact with the floor than the heel. See if you can notice some sensation from part of your foot in this way and focus all your attention there. (*Pauses.*)

Now I'll ask you, again, while staying focused, to notice that what you're observing now is *there* and the observer *here*. Or to put it another way: notice that thing in your foot and notice who it is who's noticing it. And that the distance, the space, is still there even though you're now inside your own body. *(Pauses.)*

Now I'll ask you to shift your focus to your own chest, stomach. See if you can discern some detail there too. Maybe your heart beating, some tension in your gut, or the sensation of your clothes against your skin. It might be a little more vague, but see if you can still find something to focus your attention on. Take your time. *(Pauses.)*

Now I'll ask you to notice that the observed thing is *there*, the observer *here*. Notice who it is that's doing the noticing. And notice the space. *(Pauses.)*

Now there's one more thing I'd like you to notice. It might be even more vague, but that's fine. I'd like you to notice some thoughts or images that pop into your mind. Maybe you can count some? And again: notice what comes and goes. And notice who it is who's noticing this.

So far, the exercise has been employed with material that has no specific connection with Andrew's problem. It can, however, be steered toward more personal relevance:

Therapist: I'm wondering, when you're sitting here, if you can notice something in yourself that has something to do with "The Repulsive Failure." Some thoughts, some physical sensation? Some images? *(Pauses.)* If you can, do so. Don't dive down into it; just notice again that what you're observing is *there* and you the observer are *here*. Note those images, sensations, thoughts, or physical reactions. And note who it is who's noticing them.

In the exercise, the actual distance between the observer and the observed in its earlier sequences is used as a source and the experience of the client's own reactions (physical, mental) as a target, all to train him in establishing an observational distance from his own responses in order to eventually change how certain responses affect his future behavior.

The above exercise is very much therapist-led, even though the very point is for the client to also act, albeit beyond the therapist's insight. It is therefore imperative that the therapist follow up by querying the client about his experience. The following is a possible dialogue:

Andrew: That was really strange. And hard, at times, too.

Therapist: Yes, it can be hard to talk about vague things like this. Much of what I was saying was an attempt to indicate things, to make you notice certain things. Like that distance or space between you as an observer and whatever it was I asked you to observe. Were you able to do that, do you think?

Andrew: I think so. It was as if I was standing beside myself, somehow. It was harder with thoughts, though, there at the end. My mind just went blank.

Therapist: And who was it noticing this blankness?

Andrew: (chuckling) Yeah, well, me. And it was easier with the foot. It was clearer to me than the stomach thing.

Therapist: Okay. And there was someone there noticing the difference, right?

Andrew: Me again, yeah.

The following variant exercise serves the same purpose: to help Andrew establish an observational distance from his distressing responses so that their influence over other aspects of his behavior might change.

Andrew: Everything that's happened, all the repulsive stuff, has kind of stuck to me, you know. I'm the repulsive one.

Therapist: Is it there now? Do you notice it when we're sitting here?

Andrew:	Yeah. It's not so obvious, but sure. It's almost always with me.
Therapist:	Can you do something that makes it stronger or more distinct?
Andrew:	You mean right now?
Therapist:	Yes.
Andrew:	If I think about certain things, what it was like when I was a kid with my neighbor. What he did to me.
Therapist:	Would it be okay to think about it here and now? You don't have to dig into all the details of the memory right now, but just to make clearer contact with that feeling of being repulsive so that we can see if we can work with it?
Andrew:	(*noticeably tense and stressed*) Yeah, well it's already here, simply by virtue of the fact we're talking about it. Fuck!
Therapist:	If you leave the actual memory for a moment, can you focus on what it does to you physically right now?
Andrew:	It makes me feel sick. My guts get all knotted up.
Therapist:	Is it most obvious in the guts? What about other parts of your body?
Andrew:	I can feel it pressing against my chest too, but it's mostly that tightness in my belly.
Therapist:	If this tightness had a color, what color would it be?
Andrew:	Green. A disgusting green color.
Therapist:	Shall we see if we can do different things with this green tightness? For instance, can you imagine grabbing it with your hands and placing it here on the table?
Andrew:	I don't know. Sounds weird. And I don't want to touch it.

Therapist: How about imagining that you've got special gloves? Try putting on the gloves and then put it here on the table. You can have it back in a second. Just see if you can…

Andrew: Okay. I can see it on the table.

Therapist: What does it look like?

Andrew: Like one of those plastic joke piles of vomit.

Therapist: How much of the table does it cover, this vomit, this green tightness in your belly?

Andrew: A quarter of it, maybe. In the corner closest to me.

Therapist: Is it moving in any way?

Andrew: No, it's just sitting there in a pile.

Therapist: Temperature?

Andrew: Cold.

Therapist: Can you move it? Lift it up, for example?

Andrew: Yeah, I could throw it away somewhere. That'd be nice.

Therapist: Where to?

Andrew: Into the bin there (*pointing*).

Therapist: To get rid of it. Okay. But if I've understood you correctly, it usually doesn't disappear. Or at least if it goes away it comes right back pretty soon after.

Andrew: That's right.

Therapist: So we've got it on the table. Can you kind of toss it around without trying to throw it away?

Andrew: Yeah, I can, actually. It loses some of its power.

The above is just an example of what can be done. The fundamental principle is simple: Ask questions, in the context of the exercise, that enable the client to metaphorically interact with his own distressing responses as if they were physical objects in the external world. This becomes skills training in establishing an observational distance. The questions are asked to encourage flexibility in the learning process and in different ways of interacting with the matter at hand.

In the above example, the therapist opted to focus on particular parts of the emotional and physical aspects of her client's experience—not to avoid the rest, but to help Andrew to establish an observational distance. The same fundamental principle can be used for the entire mnemonic sequence that Andrew finds so distressing.

Therapist:	I know a way we could approach what you remember, what your neighbor did. Would that be okay?
Andrew:	I don't know if I'll be able to handle it. It'll paralyze me. I'll break down.
Therapist:	Yet the memories are already here, aren't they, just through us talking about them?
Andrew:	Sure, I guess so…
Therapist:	How about doing this? You don't have to go into everything at this point, just take what's already here. Now try to project it as an image on that door there (*pointing*). Could you do that? Just the stuff you can already see.
Andrew:	I suppose I can.
Therapist:	Can you see it on the door?
Andrew:	Yes.
Therapist:	Where on the door is it? Does it cover the whole door?
Andrew:	No, just the upper half.
Therapist:	Can you move it? You know, if it came from a projector, you could move the image. Bring the image down to the bottom half of the door, for example. Can you do that?

The therapist understands that Andrew's problem is the way he interacts with his distressing memories, and sets up the therapeutic situation in order to help him distinguish between himself as actor and the content of his distressing narrative. There are many things that can be done within the parameters of the above exercise. The therapist can move in and out of the memories, home in on certain mnemonic details, and ask questions that make it more likely that Andrew will change his way of interacting with them. He can regard them at a distance and up close. The therapist can help Andrew by drawing attention to details that he had been overlooking from the inflexibility of his particular perspective. In short: by encouraging Andrew to approach his own reactions as if they were being played out at a distance (like a film projected onto a door) the therapist can help him establish an observational distance that changes their influence over the rest of his behavior. Within the frame of the exercise the therapist can do everything she would normally do during classic exposure therapy; in fact, the entire process can be seen as a variant form of exposure therapy with the addition of questions specifically formulated to establish a greater observational distance—questions, in other words, that could have been asked about an actual film. Such as:

"Is what you're looking at a simple slide or a motion picture?"

"Is it in color or in black and white?"

"Can you freeze the movie?"

"Can you play the sequence backward?"

"Can you zoom in on some detail that you hadn't noticed before?"

Experiential Exercise with Barry

Barry describes his pain and the message it is giving him: There's no point, give up! The following is an exercise that can be used to illustrate how such well-trained self-instructions operate and how a client can act with greater flexibility than he has hitherto learned.

> *Therapist:*   I've got an exercise on what to do when particular rules crop up, certain thoughts or feelings that we're used to following. Would it be okay to try it?

Barry: Sure.

Therapist: Stand up. *(She stands beside Barry.)* In this exercise, you're yourself and I'm your history. I'll tell you to do things you've learned to do and you'll experiment with what you can do, given that you have this history saying what it says. Let's assume that the actual task that you can experiment with is this: I want you to take a step forward first. One foot and then the other *(demonstrating).*

Barry: Okay.

Therapist: Let's now assume that you have a history that's given you this following rule: Always lead with your right foot! I don't know why this is, but let's just say it's the case. And I'm your history, so this is what I'm going to tell you to do. Right foot first! It'll then be time for you to take your steps and to experiment. If it's okay, you can start by simply doing what your history tells you to do. Do you understand what I want you to do?

Barry: I think so.

Therapist: Off you go, then! *(And with emphasis)* Remember, right foot first!

              (Barry takes a step forward, putting his right foot down first.)

Therapist: Do you want to try a few more times? But remember: *(with emphasis)* right foot first!

              (Barry takes a step forward, again putting his right foot down first.)

Therapist: Let me ask you a few things. Who is it that hears what your history tells you?

Barry: Me.

Therapist:	Exactly. And who is it moving the feet?
Barry:	Me.
Therapist:	So far you've moved your feet just as your history tells you to do. Now let's see if you can experiment. It's obvious you can follow the advice of your history. So you still can, if you want. You can lead with your right foot. Shall we see if you can do something different? But let me warn you: I'm your history and I'll tell you what I always tell you. Right foot first!
	(Barry stands still, hesitating, and the therapist repeats with emphasis: "Right foot first!" Barry takes a few steps, but this time leading with his left foot.)
Therapist:	How was that?
Barry:	It felt pretty weird, actually. Like I had to really concentrate first.
Therapist:	And who is it who took note of this weird feeling?
Barry:	Me.
Therapist:	And who's moving your feet?
Barry:	Me.

The therapist and Barry repeat the task a few more times, with the therapist emphasizing the same instruction and asking the same questions about who it is that is taking note of what, and who is acting. The therapist then concludes the exercise and invites Barry's reflections. Could he relate to the exercise? One way of clarifying its intended point is to say:

"Here we had a silly little rule about which foot to lead with. It's hardly a problem in your real life. But what about other rules that are only too ready to govern your steps, such as 'there's no point; give up'?"

As in the postlude to all experiential exercises, it is valuable to ask clients about what they experience, and because the responses you get will differ from one person to the next, this dialogue can take different forms. A fairly common experience in this particular exercise is that "doing what my history tells me to" is very automatic and surprisingly powerful. Many clients also refer to the rather peculiar experience of "choosing." That we can actually do precisely that, even in the presence of ingrained self-rules, is one of the main points of the exercise.

What is it the therapist is trying to do in terms of the three principles?

- **Functional analysis:** The client's habitual compliance with an ingrained instruction or rule is illustrated and intended as an application of a functional analysis of a dysfunctional behavioral strategy. In the possibility of choice, the idea is to place the client in experiential contact with an alternative strategy.

- **Establishing an observational distance:** The extreme simplification of the dysfunctional strategy (and its alternative) is intended to increase the likelihood of an increased observational distance.

- **Clarifying what is important in life and what concrete steps can be taken in that direction:** As the exercise has been described so far, there is no obvious connection with this therapeutic principle. But the dialogue is easy to steer there, given that Barry experiences "the opportunity to choose" within the context of the exercise, spurred by questions like, "If you could choose, in areas where you have previously simply done what you history has told you to, what would be important for you to do?"

If Barry can relate to the exercise, this simplification can allow the therapist (and Barry himself) to use it as a metaphor when the need arises—perhaps when Barry again describes one of the self-rules that readily traps him, and says something like, "There's no point. I might as well give up." In this case, a possible comment is "Right foot first!"

The reader presumably understands these exercises to be metaphorical. Clients in psychological therapy have no problem walking along a line on the floor in the face of written impediments, or of leading with their left foot. There is no actual distance between a person and thoughts that person has. The experience of disgust has no color and cannot be placed on a table. A memory is not a film that can be projected onto a door. However, if these exercises work metaphorically they can be used for effecting change, in accordance with the three principles highlighted in this book.

Afterword

My strategy in this book has been to unify basic research with psychotherapeutic practice to see if any light can be shed on an area that most psychotherapeutic models deem important—namely, how metaphors can be used in conversations that are intended to help people toward change. To this end, I've used research from two somewhat different disciplines, linguistics and behavior analysis, which have proved to have either remarkably similar or complementary standpoints on our scientific understanding of how metaphors are used in human interaction.

I have then gone from a fundamental understanding of metaphor use in general to psychotherapeutic practice, using three principles based on behavior analysis—in particular a modern behavior analysis of language and cognition known as relational frame theory. The outcome is a series of proposals for how metaphors can be used in conversations intended to effect change. It is my hope that these proposals will help both therapists and researchers in their endeavours to ascertain how conversations, and particularly the use of metaphors in such conversations, can contribute to whatever changes people seek for themselves.

Metaphors About Science

What in everyday parlance we call "literal language" has been pushed backstage in this book. As I pointed out earlier, this is not because this way of speaking is in any sense unimportant; indeed, in many situations it performs a particular, critical function. One such situation is scientific talk and what we call theories. Here, the vagueness that characterizes metaphorical talk is often a disadvantage. In scientific theory you want maximum precision and accuracy, as far as possible. This is why, for instance, the description of RFT, which is the scientific keystone of this book, tries to be technical and precise rather than metaphorically expressive. At the same time, metaphors fulfill a function here too, namely as pointers oriented toward some central feature. The term "relational framing" is itself an example of this. It is a metaphor intended to orient the listener toward the idea that we "frame" everything we encounter by relating it to other things. We, as partakers of a social community, establish the relations.

I began this book by mentioning some Swedish poets, and now intend to close by handing it over to another—Thomas Tidholm. I do so because I think that the following makes a particularly apposite statement about my scientific point of departure: functional contextualism. The poem points to something pivotal to this book. So, in closing, it's back to basics.

Where from?

I know many people wonder where it comes from, whether from inside or outside, and if it could run out. I say it comes from the outside. You can tell by our hands, how we hold them out ready to receive it. Our entire being is turned that way, face and all.

Nothing is turned inwards, only the back. You don't expect anything from there, that's why there is no face on that side. You can laugh there, but your laugh comes out through your mouth and goes to meet whatever comes from the outside, to say hello, and bring it inside.

Some people say that we stretch out our hands or laugh in order to give away what we have, but that's not what I think. I think we just want more and more, always more. I don't think we have anything.

Then they ask if it can run out.
I say it cannot. That at least is for sure.
It lasts your whole life.

Thomas Tidholm, 1991
Translated by Gabriella Berggren

Acknowledgments

From the days of my earliest thought on writing something about metaphor and psychotherapy until today, almost twenty years have passed. I can look back on a rich journey, and many collegues and friends have contributed to what is now this book, some by their research and others through creative dialogue. Some know that they contributed, others probably not. I will forever remain grateful to so many. As for the English version, a special thank-you to Carmen Luciano, Fran Ruiz, Ian Stewart, and Matthieu Villatte, who have read all or parts of the manuscript and made many vaulable suggestions. All deficiences remain, of course, my own responsibility. Thank you also to Neil Betteridge, who did most of the translation from Swedish to English, and to Susan LaCroix for her smooth way of editing the final version.

Finally, I want to acknowledge a large group of people whom I cannot mention by name. The many clients I have seen over the years have taught me so much, not least by the way in which they have used metaphor. A big, warm thank-you to one and all!

References

Amrhein, P. C. (2004). How does motivational interviewing work? What client talk reveals. *Journal of cognitive psychotherapy: An international quarterly, 18*, 323–336.

Angus, L. E. (1996). An intensive analysis of metaphor themes in psychotherapy. In J. S. Mio (ed.), *Metaphor: Implications and applications*. Mahvah, NJ: Lawrence Erlbaum Associates.

Angus, L. E., & Greenberg, L. S. (2011). *Working with narrative in emotion-focused therapy: Changing stories, healing lives*. Washington: American Psychological Association.

Angus, L. E., & Korman, Y. (2002). Conflict, coherence and change in brief psychotherapy: A metaphor theme analysis. In S. R. Russel (ed.), *The verbal communication of emotions: Interdisciplinary perspectives*. Mahvah, NJ: Lawrence Erlbaum Associates.

Angus, L. E., & Rennie, D. L. (1988). Therapist participation in metaphor generation: Collaborative and noncollaborative styles. *Psychotherapy, 25*, 552–560.

Angus, L. E., & Rennie, D. L. (1989). Envisioning the representational world: The client's experience of metaphoric expression in psychotherapy. *Psychotherapy, 26*, 372–379.

Aristotle (1920). *The poetics*. Oxford: The Clarendon Press.

Barker, P. (1985). *Using metaphors in psychotherapy*. New York: Brunner.

Barlow, D. H. (2002). *Anxiety and its disorders: The nature and treatment of anxiety and panic* (2nd ed.). New York: Guilford Press.

Barlow, D. H., Farchione, T. J., Fairholme, C. P., Ellard, K. K., Boisseau, C. L., Allen, L. B., & Ehrenreich, M. (2010). *Unified protocol for transdiagnostic treatment of emotional disorders: Therapist guide*. New York: Oxford University Press

Barlow, D. H. (red.). (2014). *Clinical handbook of psychological disorders* (5ᵗʰ ed.) New York: Guilford Press.

Barnes-Holmes, D., & Stewart, I. (2004). Relational frame theory and analogical reasoning: Empirical investigations. *International Journal of Psychology and Psychological Therapy, 4*, 241–262.

Bateman, A., & Fonagy, P. (2006). *Mentalization based treatment of borderline personality disorder: A practical guide.* Oxford: Oxford University Press.

Battino, R. (2002). *Metaphoria: Metaphor and guided metaphor for psychotherapy and healing.* Carmarthen: Crown House Publishing Ltd.

Beck, A. T. (1976). *Cognitive therapy and the emotional disorders.* New York: Meredian.

Beck, A. T., & Weishaar, M. (1989). Cognitive therapy. In A. Freeman, K. M. Simon, L. E. Beutler, & H. Arkowitz (ed.), *Comprehensive handbook of cognitive therapy* (s. 21–36). New York: Plenum Press.

Bennet-Levi, J., Butler, G., Fennel, M., Hackman, A., Mueller, M., & Westbrook, D. (2004). *Oxford guide to behavioural experiments in cognitive therapy.* Oxford: Oxford University Press.

Bernstein, A., Hadash, Y., Lichtash, Y., Tanay, G., Shepherd, K., & Fresco, D. M. (2015). Decentering and related contructs: A critical review and metacognitive processes model. *Perspectives on Psychological Science, 10*, 599–617.

Billow, R. M. (1977). Metaphor: A review of the psychological literature. *Psychological Bulletin, 84*, 81–92.

Bleiberg, K. L., & Markowitz, J. C. (2014). Interpersonal psychotherapy for depression. In D. H. Barlow (ed.), *Clinical handbook of psychological disorders* (5ᵗʰ ed.) (p. 332–352). New York: Guilford Press.

Blenkiron, P. (2010). *Stories and analogies in cognitive behaviour therapy.* Chichester: Wiley-Blackwell.

Bond, F. W., Hayes, S. C., Baer, R. A., Carpenter, K. M., Guenole, N., Orcutt, H. K., Watz, T., & Zettle, R. D. (2011). Preliminary psychometric properties of the acceptance and action questionnaire-II: A revised measure of psychological inflexibility and experiential avoidance. *Behavior Therapy, 42*, 676–688.

Boroditsky, L. (2000). Metaphoric structuring: Understanding time through spatial metaphors. *Cognition, 22,* 1–28.

Boroditsky, L. (2001). Does language shape thought? English and Mandarin speakers' conceptions of time. *Cognitive Psychology, 43,* 1–22.

Boroditsky, L., Schmidt, L. A., & Phillips, W. (2003). Sex, syntax and semantics. In D. Gentner & S. Goldin-Meadow (ed.), *Language in mind: Advances in language and cognition* (p. 61–79). Boston: MIT Press.

Brennan, S. E., & Clark, H. H. (1996). Conceptual pacts and lexical choice in conversation. *Journal of Experimental psychology: Learning, Memory and Cognition, 22,* 1482–1493.

Bryan, C. J., Ray-Sannerud, B., & Heron, E. A. (2015). Psychological flexibility as a dimension of resilience for posttraumatic stress, depression, and risk for suicidal ideation among Air Force personnel. *Journal of Contextual Behavioral Science, 4,* 263–268.

Cardillo, E. R., Watson, C. E., Schmidt, G. L., Kranjec, A., & Chatterje, A. (2012). From novel to familiar: Tuning the brain for metaphors. *Neuroimage, 59,* 3212–3221.

Catania, A. C. (2007). *Learning* (4th ed.). New York: Sloan Publishing.

Chawla, N., & Ostafin, B. (2007). Experiential avoidance as a functional dimensional approach to psychopathology: An empirical review. *Journal of Clinical Psychology, 63,* 871–890.

Chemero, A. (2009). *Radical embodied cognitive science.* Cambridge: The MIT Press.

Christoffer, P. J., & Dougher, M. J. (2009) A behavior analytic account of motivational interviewing. *The Behavior Analyst, 32,* 149–161.

Ciarrochi, J., Bilich, L., & Godsel, C. (2010). Psychological flexibility as a mechanism of change in acceptance and commitment therapy. In R. Baer. *Assessing mindfulness and acceptance: Illuminating the processes of change* (p. 51–76). Oakland. New Harbinger Publications.

Cienki, A., & Müller, C. (2008). Metaphor, gesture and thought. In R. W. Gibbs (red.), *The Cambridge handbook of metaphor and thought* (p. 483–501). New York: Cambridge University Press.

Clark, D. M., Ehlers, A., Hackmann, A., McManus, F., Fennell, M., Grey, N., et al. (2006). Cognitive therapy versus exposure and applied relaxation in social phobia: A randomized controlled trial. *Journal of consulting and clinical psychology, 74,* 568–578.

Combs, G., & Freedman, J. (1990). *Symbol, story and ceremony: Using metaphor in individual and family therapy.* New York: W. W. Norton & Company.

Coulson, S. (2008). Metaphor comprehension and the brain. In R. W. Gibbs (ed.), *The Cambridge handbook of metaphor and thought* (p. 177–194). New York: Cambridge University Press.

Craske, M. G., & Barlow, D. H. (2014). Panic disorder and agarophobia. In D. H. Barlow (red.), (2014). *Clinical handbook of psychological disorders* (5th ed.) (p. 1–61). New York: Guilford Press.

Craske, M. G., Treanor, M., Conway, C. C., Zbozinek, T., & Vervliet, B. (2014). Maximizing exposure therapy: An inhibitory learning approach. *Behavior research and therapy, 58,* 10–23.

Dahl, J. C., Plumb, J. C., Stewart, I., & Lundgren, T. (2009). *The art & science of valuing in psychotherapy.* Oakland: New Harbinger Publications.

Dimidjian, S., Martell, C. R., Herman-Dunn, R., & Hubley, S. (2014). Behavioral activation for depression. In D. H. Barlow (ed.) *Clinical handbook of psychological disorders* (5th ed.) (p. 353–393). New York: Guilford Press.

Dymond, S., & Roche, B. (2013). *Advances in relational frame theory: Research and application.* Oakland: New Harbinger Publications.

Fausey, C. M., & Boroditsky, L. (2011). Who dunnit? Cross-linguistic differences in eye-witness memory. *Psychonomic Bulletin & Review, 18,* 150–157.

Fedden, S., & Boroditsky, L. (2012). Spatialization of time in Mian. doi: 10.3369/fpsyg.2012.00485

Flückiger, C., Del Re, A. C., Wampold, B. E., Symonds, D., & Horvath, A. O. (2011). How central is the alliance in psychotherapy? A multilevel longitudinal meta-analysis. *Journal of consulting psychology, 59,* 10–17.

Foa, E. B., Hembree, E. A., & Rothbaum, B. O. (2007). *Prolonged exposure for PTSD: Emotional processing of traumatic experiences.* Oxford: Oxford University Press.

Foa, E. B., Huppert, J. D., & Cahill, S. P. (2006). Emotional processing theory: An update. In Rothbaum, B. O (ed.), *Pathological anxiety: Emotional processing in etiology and treatment* (p. 3–24). New York: Guilford Press.

Foody, M., Barnes-Holmes, Y., Barnes-Holmes, D., & Luciano, C. (2013). An empirical investigation of hierarchical versus distinction relations in a self-based ACT exercise. *International journal of psychology and psychological therapy, 13,* 373–385.

Foody, M., Barnes-Holmes, Y., Barnes-Holmes, D., Rai, L., & Luciano, C. (2015). An empirical investigation of the role of self, hierarchy and distinction in a common ACT exercise. *Psychological record, 65,* 231–243.

Foody, M., Barnes-Holmes, Y., Barnes-Holmes, D., Törneke, N., Luciano, C., Stewart, I., & McEnteggart, C. (2014). RFT for clinical use: The example of metaphor. *Journal of contextual behavioral science, 3,* 305–313.

Forceville, C. (2009). Non-verbal and multimodal metaphor in a cognitivist framework: Agendas for research. In C. J. Forceville & E. Urio-Aparisi (ed.), *Multimodal metaphor* (p. 19–42). Berlin: Mouton de Gruyfer.

Franklin, M. E., & Foa, E. B. (2014). Obsessive-compulsive disorder. In D. H. Barlow (ed.), *Clinical handbook of psychological* disorders (5th ed.) (p. 155–205). New York: Guilford Press.

Fryling, M. (2013). Constructs and events in verbal behavior. *The analysis of verbal behavior, 29,* 157–165.

Fuhrman, O., McGormick, K., Chen, E., Jiang, H., Shu, D., Mao, S., & Boroditsky, L. (2011). How linguistic and cultural forces shape conceptions of time: English and Mandarin time in 3D. *Cognitive science, 35,* 1305–1328.

Gentner, D., & Bowdle, B. (2008). Metaphor as structure-mapping. In R. W. Gibbs (ed.), *The Cambridge handbook of metaphor and thought* (p. 109–128). New York: Cambridge University Press.

Gibbs R. W. (red.). (2008). *The Cambridge handbook of metaphor and thought.* New York: Cambridge University Press.

Gifford, E. V., & Hayes, S. C. (1999). Functional contextualism: A pragmatic philosophy for behavioral science. In W. O'Donohue & R. Kitchener (ed.), *Handbook of behaviorism* (p. 285–327). San Diego: Academic Press.

Gil-Luciano, B., Ruiz, F. J., Valdivia-Salas, S., & Suárez-Falcón, J. C. (2016) Promoting psychological flexibility on tolerance tasks: Framing behaviour through deictic/hierarchical relations and specifying augmental functions. *The psychological record* doi:10.1007/s40732–016–0200–5.

Giora, R. (2008). Is metaphor unique? In R. W. Gibbs (ed.), *The Cambridge handbook of metaphor and thought* (p. 143–160) NY: Cambridge University Press.

Gloster, A. T., Klotsche, J., Chaker, S., Hummel, K. V., & Hoyer, J. (2011). Assessing psychological flexibility: What does it add above and beyond existing constructs? *Psychological assessment, 23,* 970–982.

Greenberg, L. S., & Pavio, S. C. (1997). *Working with emotions in psychotherapy.* New York: Guilford Press.

Greenberg, L. S., Rice, L. N., & Elliot, R. (1993). *Fascilitating emotional change: The moment by moment process.* New York: Guilford Press.

Hayes, L. J. (1994). Thinking. In L. Hayes, S. C. Hayes, O. Kochi, & M. Sato (eds.), *Behavior analysis of language and cognition.* (p. 149–164) Oakland, CA: New Harbinger Publications.

Hayes, L. J. (1998). Remembering as a psychological event. *Journal of theoretical and philosophical psychology, 18,* 135–143.

Hayes, S. C. (1997). Behavioral epistemology includes nonverbal knowing. In L. J. Hayes & P. M. Ghezzi, (ed.) *Investigations in behavioral epistemology* (p. 35–43). Reno: Context Press.

Hayes S. C., Barnes-Holmes, D., & Roche, B. (red.). (2001). *Relational frame theory: A post Skinnerian account of human language and cognition.* New York: Kluwer Academic/Plenum Publishers.

Hayes, S. C., Strosahl, K., & Wilson, K. G. (2012). *Acceptance and commitment therapy. The process and practice of mindful change.* New York: Guilford Press.

Hayes, S. C., Wilson, K. G., Gifford, E. V., Follette, V. M., & Strosahl, K. (1996). Experiential avoidance and behavioral disorders: A functional dimensional approach to diagnosis and treatment. *Journal of consulting and clinical psychology, 64,* 1152–1168.

Hearn, J., & Lawrence, M. (1981). Family sculpting: I. Some doubts and some possibilities. *Journal of family therapy, 3,* 341–352.

Horvath, A. O., Del Re, A. C., Flückiger, C., & Symonds, D. (2011). Alliance in individual psychotherapy. In J. C. Norcross (ed.), *Psychotherapy relationships that work* (p. 25–69). Oxford: Oxford University Press.

Hughes, S., & Barnes-Holmes, D. (2016). Relational frame theory: The basic account. In S. C. Hayes, D. Barnes-Holmes, R. Zettle, & T. Biglan (red.), *The Wiley handbook of contextual behavioral science* (p. 129–179). Chichester: John Wiley & Sons.

Karp, M., & Holmes, P. (1998). *The handbook of psychodrama*. London: Routledge.

Kashdan, T. B., Barrios, V., Forsyth, J. P., & Steger, M. F. (2006). Experiential avoidance as a generalized psychological vulnerability: Comparisons with coping and emotion regulation strategies. *Behaviour research and therapy, 9*, 1301–1320.

Kashdan, T. B., & Rottenberg, J. (2010). Psychological flexibility as a fundamental aspect of health. *Clinical psychology review, 30*, 865–878.

Katz, S. M. (2013). *Metaphor and fields: Common ground, common language and the future of psychoanalysis*. New York: Routledge.

Kohlenberg, R. J., & Tsai, M. (1991). *Functional analytical psychotherapy: Creating intense and curative therapeutic relationships*. New York: Plenum.

Kopp, R. R. (1995). *Metaphor therapy: Using client-generated metaphors in psychotherapy*. New York: Brunner/Mazel.

Kopp, R. R., & Craw, M. J. (1998). Metaphoric language, metaphoric cognition and cognitive therapy. *Psychotherapy 35*, 306–311.

Kövecses, Z. (2002). Emotion concepts: Social constructivism and cognitive linguistics. In S. R. Fussell (ed.), *The verbal communications of emotions: Interdisciplinary perspectives* (p. 109–124). Mahwak, NJ: Lawrence Erlbaum Associates Inc.

Kövecses, Z. (2010). *Metaphor: A practical introduction*. New York: Oxford University.

Lakoff, G. (1993). The contemporary theory of metaphor. In A. Ortony (ed.), *Metaphor and thought* (second ed.) (p. 202–251). Cambridge: Cambridge University Press.

Lakoff, G. (2008). The neural theory of metaphor. In R. W. Gibbs (red.) *The Cambridge handbook of metaphor and thought* (p. 17–38). New York: Cambridge University Press.

Lakoff, G., & Johnson, M. (1980). *Metaphors we live by.* Chicago: University of Chicago Press.

Lang, T., & Helbig-Lang, S. (2012). Exposure in vivo with and without presence of a therapist: Does it matter? In P. Neudeck, H-U. Wittchen (ed.), *Exposure therapy: Rethinking the model—refining the method* (p. 261–273). New York: Springer Science.

Lawley, J., & Tompkins, P. (2000). *Metaphors in mind: Transformation through symbolic modelling.* London: The Developing Company Press.

Leary, D. E. (1990). Psyche's muse: the role of metaphor in the history of psychology. In Leary, D. E. (ed.), *Metaphors in the history of psychology* (p. 1–23) New York: Cambridge University Press.

Legowski, T. & Brownlee, K. (2001). Working with metaphor in narrative therapy. *Journal of family psychotherapy, 12,* 19–28.

Levin, M. E., Luoma, J. B., Vilardaga, R., Lillis, J., Nobles, R., & Hayes, S. C. (2015). Examining the role of psychological inflexibility, perspective taking, and emphatic concern in generalized prejudice. *Journal of applied social psychology, 46,* 180–191.

Levin, M. E., MacLane, C., Daflos, S., Seeley, J. R., Hayes, S. C., Biglan, A., & Pistorello, J. (2014). Examining psychological inflexibility as a transdiagnostic process across psychological disorders. *Journal of contextual behavioral science, 3,* 155–163.

Levitt, H., Korman, Y., & Angus, L. (2000). A metaphor analysis in treatments of depression: Metaphor as a marker of change. *Counselling psychology quarterly, 13,* 23–35.

Linehan, M. M. (1993). *Cognitive-behavioral treatment of borderline personality disorder.* New York: Guilford Press.

Linehan, M. M. (1997). Validation and psychotherapy. In. A. C. Bohart & L. S. Greenberg (ed.), *Empathy reconsidered: New directions in psychotherapy* (p. 353–392). Washington, DC: American Psychological Association.

Linehan, M. M. (2015). *The DBT skills training manual* (second ed.). New York: Guilford Press.

Lipkens, R., & Hayes, S. C. (2009). Producing and recognizing analogical relations. *Journal of experimental analysis of behavior, 91,* 105–126.

Longmore, R., & Worrel, M. (2007). Do we need to challenge thoughts in cognitive behavior therapy? *Clinical psychology review, 27,* 173–187.

Luciano, C., Ruiz, F. J., Vizcaino-Torres, R. M., Sánches-Martin, V., Martinez, O., & Lópes-Lópes, J. C. (2011). A relational frame analysis of defusion in acceptance and commitment therapy. *International journal of psychology and psychological therapy, 11,* 165–182.

Luciano, C., Valdivia-Salas, S., Cabello-Luque, F., & Hernández, M. (2009).

Developing self-directed rules. In R. A. Rehfeldt & Y. Barnes-Holmes (ed.), *Derived relational responding: Applications for learners with autism and other developmental disabilities* (p. 335–352). Oakland: New Harbinger Publications.

Lundahl, B., & Burke, B. L. (2009). The effectiveness and applicability of motivational interviewing: A practice friendly review of four meta-analyses. *Journal of clinical psychology. In session, 65,* 1232–1245.

Martell, C. R., Addis, M. E., & Jacobson, N. S. (2001). *Depression in context: Strategies for guided action.* New York: W. W. Norton.

Martin, J., Cummings, A. L., & Hallberg E. T. (1992) Therapists' intentional use of metaphor: Memorability, clinical impact and possible epistemic/ motivational functions. *Journal of consulting and clinical psychology, 60,* 143–145.

McCullough, L., Kuhn, N., Andrews, S., Kaplan, A., Wolf, J., & Lanza Hurley, C. L. (2003). *Treating affect phobia: A manual for short-term dynamic psychotherapy.* New York: Guilford Press.

McHugh, L., & Stewart, I. (2012). *The self and perspective taking: Contributions and applications from modern behavioral science.* Oakland: New Harbinger Publications.

McCurry, S. M., & Hayes, S. C. (1992) Clinical and experimental perspectives on metaphorical talk. *Clinical psychology review, 12,* 763–785.

McMullen, L. M. (1989) Use of figurative language in successful and unsuccessful cases of psychotherapy: Three comparisons. *Metaphor and symbolic activity, 4,* 203–225.

McMullen, L. M. (2008). Putting it in context: Metaphor and psychotherapy. In R. W. Gibbs (red.), *The Cambridge handbook of metaphor and thought* (p. 397–411). New York: Cambridge University Press.

McMullen, L. M., & Convey, J. B. (2002). Conventional metaphors for depression. In S. R. Russel (ed.), *The verbal communication of emotions: Interdisciplinary perspectives* (p. 167–182) Mahvah, NJ: Lawrence Erlbaum Associates.

Mennin, D. S., Ellard, K. K., Fresco D. M., & Gross, J. J. (2013) United we stand: Emphasizing commonalities across cognitive-behavioral therapies. *Behavior therapist, 44,* 234–248.

Miller, W. R., & Rollnick, S. (2013). *Motivational interviewing: helping people change.* New York: Guilford Press.

Miller, W. R., & Rose, G. S. (2009). Toward a theory of motivational interviewing. *American psychologist, 64,* 527–537.

Monson, C. M., Resick, P. A., & Rizvi, S. L. (2014). Posttraumatic stress disorder. In D. H. Barlow (ed.), *Clinical handbook of psychological disorders* (5th ed.) (p. 62–114). New York: Guilford Press.

Morris, M. W., Sheldon, O. J., Ames, D. R., & Young, M. J. (2007). Metaphors and the market: Consequences and preconditions of agent and object metaphors in stock market commentary. *Organizational behavior and human decision processes. 102,* 174–192.

Müller, C. (2008). *Metaphors dead and alive, sleeping and walking: A dynamic view.* Chicago: University of Chicago Press.

Müller, C., & Cienki, A (2009). Words, gestures and beyond: Forms of multimodal metaphor in the use of spoken language. In C. J. Forceville & E. Urio-Aparisi (ed.), *Multimodal metaphor* (p. 297–328). Berlin: Mouton de Gruyfer.

Muran, J. C., & DiGiuseppe, R. A. (1990.) Toward a cognitive formulation of metaphor use in psychotherapy. *Clinical psychology review, 10,* 69–85.

Neacsiu, A. D., & Linehan, M. M. (2014). Borderline personality disorder. In D. H. Barlow (ed.), *Clinical handbook of psychological disorders* (5 uppl.) (p. 394–461). New York: Guilford Press.

Needham-Didsbury, I. (2014). Metaphor in psychotherapeutic discourse: Implications for utterance interpretation. *Poznan studies in contemporary linguistics, 50,* 75–97.

Neudeck, P., & Einsle, F. (2012). Dissemination of exposure therapy in clinical practice: How to handle the barriers? In P. Neudeck & H.-U. Wittchen (eds.), *Exposure therapy: Rethinking the model—refining the method* (p. 23–34). New York: Springer Science.

Neudeck, P., & Wittchen, H.-U. (2012). *Exposure therapy: Rethinking the model—refining the method.* New York: Springer Science.

Noë, A. (2004). *Action in perception.* Cambridge: The MIT Press.

Norcross, J. C., & Lampert, M. J. (2011). Psychotherapy relationships that work II. *Psychotherapy, 48,* 4–8.

Ogden, P., & Fisher, J. (2015) *Sensimotor psychotherapy: interventions for trauma and attachment.* New York: W. W. Norton & Company.

Ogden, P., Pain, C., & Fisher, J. (2006). A sensorimotor approach to the treatment of trauma and dissociation. *Psychiatric clinics of North America, 29,* 263–279.

Ollendick, T. H., & Davis, T. E. (2013). One session treatment for specific phobias: A review of Öst's single-session exposure with children and adolescents. *Cognitive behavioral therapy, 42,* 275–283.

Ortony, A. (1993). Metaphor, language and thought. In A. Ortony (ed.), *Metaphor and thought* (p. 1–16) (second ed.) Cambridge: Cambridge University Press.

Payne, L. A., Ellard, K. K., Farchione, C. F., Fairholme, C. P., & Barlow, D. H. (2014). Emotional disorders: A unified transdiagnostic protocol. In D. H. Barlow (ed.), *Clinical handbook of psychological disorders* (5th ed.) (p. 237–274). New York: Guilford Press.

Porges, S. W. (2011). *The polyvagal theory. Neurophysiological foundations of emotions, attachment, communication, self-regulation.* New York: W. W. & Company.

Ramnerö, J., & Törneke, N. (2008). *The ABCs of human behavior. Behavioral principles for the practicing clinician.* Oakland: New Harbinger Publications.

Ramnerö, J., & Törneke, N. (2015). On having a goal: Goals as representations or behavior. *The psychological record, 65,* s. 89–99.

Rasmussen, B., & Angus, L. (1996). Metaphor in psychodynamic psychotherapy with borderline and none-borderline clients: A qualitative analysis. *Psychotherapy, 33,* 521–530.

Rasmussen, B. M. (2002). Linking metaphors and dreams in clinical practice. *Psychoanalytic social work, 9,* 71–87.

Ritchie, L. D. (2006). *Context and connection in metaphor.* New York: Palgrave Macmillan.

Roemer, L., & Orsillo, S. M. (2014). An acceptance-based behavioral therapy for generalized anxiety disorder. In D. H. Barlow (ed.), *Clinical handbook of psychological disorders* (5th ed.) (p. 206–236). New York: Guilford Press.

Rosen, S. (1982). *My voice will go with you: The teaching and tales of Milton. H. Erickson.* New York: W. W. Norton & Company.

Ruiz, F. J., & Luciano, C. (2011). Cross-domain analogies as relating derived relations among two separate relational networks. *Journal of the experimental analysis of behavior, 95,* 369–385.

Ruiz, F. J., & Luciano, C. (2015). Common physical properties among relational networks improve analogy aptness. *Journal of the experimental analysis of behavior, 103,* 498–510.

Safran, J. D., & Muran, J. C. (2000). *Negotiating the therapeutic alliance: A relational treatment guide.* New York: Guilford Press.

Safran J. D., & Segal, Z. D. (1990). *Interpersonal process in cognitive therapy.* New York: Guilford Press.

Schnall, S. (2014). Are there basic metaphors? In M. J. Landau, M. D. Robinson & B. P. Meier (ed.), *The power of metaphor: Examining its influence on social life* (p. 225–247). Washington: American Psychological Association.

Segal, Z. V., Williams, M. G., & Teasdale, J. D. (2001). *Mindfulness-based cognitive therapy for depression: A new approach to preventing relapse.* New York: Guilford Press.

Sierra, M. A., Ruiz, F. J., Flórez, C. L., Riaño-Hernández, D. R., & Luciano, C. (2016). The role of common physical properties and augmental functions in metaphor effect. *International Journal of Psychology and Psychological Therapy, 16,* 265–279.

Skinner, B. F. (1957). *Verbal Behavior.* New York: Appelton-Century-Crofts.

Skinner, B. F. (1974). *About behaviorism.* New York: Knopf.

Skinner, B. F. (1989). The origins of cognitive thought. *American psychologist, 44,* 13–18.

Steen, G. J. (2011) The contemporary theory of metaphor—now new and improved. *Review of cognitive linguistics, 9:1,* 26–64.

Stewart, I., & Barnes-Holmes, D. (2001). Understanding metaphor: A relational frame perspective. *Behavior Analyst, 24,* 191–199.

Stewart, I., Barnes-Holmes, D., & Roche, B. (2004). A functional-analytic model of analogy using the relational evaluation procedure. *Psychological Record, 54,* 531–552.

Stewart, I., Barnes-Holmes, D., Roche, B., & Smeets, P. M. (2001). Generating derived relational networks via the abstraction of common physical properties: A possible model of analogical reasoning. *Psychological record, 51,* 381–408.

Stine, J. J. (2005). The use of metaphors in the service of the therapeutic alliance and therapeutic communication. *Journal of the American Academy of Psychoanalysis and Dynamic Psychiatry 33,* 531–545.

Stoddard, J. A., & Afari, N. (2014). *The big book of ACT metaphors.* Oakland: New Harbinger Publications.

Stott, R., Mansell, W., Salkovskis, P., Lavender, A., & Cartwright-Hatton, S. (2010). *Oxford guide to metaphors in CBT: Building cognitive bridges.* Oxford: Oxford University Press.

Sullivan, W., & Rees, J. (2008). *Clean language: Revealing metaphors and opening minds.* Carmarthen: Crown House Publishing.

Tay, D. (2013). *Metaphor in psychotherapy: A descriptive and prescriptive analysis.* Amsterdam: John Benjamins Publishing Company Teasdale.

Tay, D., (2014). Metaphor theory for counselling professionals. In J. Littlemore & J. R. Taylor (Eds.), *Bloomsbury companion to cognitive linguistics* (pp. 352–366). London: Bloomsbury.

Tay, D. (2016a) Metaphor and psychological transference. *Metaphor and Symbol 31(1),* 11–30.

Tay, D. (2016b). The nuances of metaphor theory for constructivist psychotherapy, *Journal of constructivist psychology,* DOI:10.1080/10720537.2016.116 1571.

Tay, D. (2016c) Using metaphor in healthcare: Mental health interventions. In Semino, E., & Demien, Z. (ed) *The Routledge handbook of metaphor and language.* New York: Routledge.

Tay, D., & Jordan, J. (2015). Metaphor and the notion of control in trauma talk. *Text & talk, 35*(4), 553–573.

Thibodeau, P. H., & Boroditsky, L. (2011). Metaphors we think with: The role of metaphor in reasoning. PLoS ONE 6(2): e16782. doi:10.1371/journal.pone.0016782.

Thibodeau, P. H., & Boroditsky, L. (2013). Natural language metaphors covertly influence reasoning. PLoS ONE 8(1): e52961. doi:10.1371/journal.pone.0052961.

Tidholm, T. (2005). *Outdoor life: prose & poetry.* Translated from Swedish by Gabriella Berggren. Parsley Press.

Törneke, N. (2010). *Learning RFT. An introduction to relational frame theory and its clinical application.* Oakland: New Harbinger Publications.

Törneke, N., Luciano, C., Barnes-Holmes, Y., & Bond, F. (2016). RFT for clinical practice: Three core strategies in understanding and treating human suffering. In R. D. Zettle, S. C. Hayes, D. Barnes-Holmes, & T. Biglan (ed.), *Wiley handbook of contextual behavioral science* (p. 254–272). Chichester: John Wiley & Sons.

Törneke, N., Luciano, C., & Valdivia-Salas, S. (2008). Rule-governed behavior and psychological problems. *International journal of psychology and psychological therapy, 8*(2), 141–156.

Tranströmer, T. (2011) The great enigma. *New collected poems.* Translated from Swedish by Robin Fulton. New York: New Direction Books.

Tryon, G. S., & Winograd G. (2011). Goal consensus and collaboration. *Psychotherapy, 48,* 50–57.

Villatte, M., Villatte, J. L., & Hayes, S. C. (2016). *Mastering the clinical conversation: Language as intervention.* New York: Guilford Press.

Wachtel, P. L. (2011). *Therapeutic communications: Knowing what to say when.* New York: Guilford Press.

Wee, L. (2005). Constructing the source: Metaphor as a discourse strategy. *Discourse studies, 7,* 363–384.

Weissman, M. M., Markowitz, J. C., & Klerman, G. L. (2000). *Comprehensive guide to interpersonal psychotherapy.* New York: Basic Books.

Wells, A. (2005). Detached mindfulness in cognitive therapy: A metacognitive analysis and ten techniques. *Journal of rational-emotive & cognitive-behavior therapy, 23,* 337–355.

Wilson, K. G. (2001). Some notes on theoretical constructs: Types and validation from a contextual behavioural perspective: *International journal of psychology and psychological Therapy, 1,* 205–215.

Young, J. E., Klosko, J. S., & Weishaar, M. E. (2003). *Schema therapy: A practitioner's guide.* New York: Guilford Press.

Young, J. E., Rygh, J. L., Weinberger, A. D., & Beck, A. T. (2014). Cognitive therapy for depression. In D. H. Barlow (red.) (2014), *Clinical handbook of psychological disorders* (5th ed.) (p. 275–331). New York: Guilford Press.

Yus, F. (2009). Visual metaphor versus verbal metaphor: A unified account. In C. J. Forceville & E. Urio-Aparisi (ed.), *Multimodal metaphor* (p.147–172). Berlin: Mouton de Gruyfer.

Niklas Törneke, MD, is a psychiatrist, and has worked as a senior psychiatrist in the department of general psychiatry in his hometown of Kalmar, Sweden, from 1991 until he started a private practice in 1998. He earned his license as a psychotherapist in 1996, and was originally trained as a cognitive therapist. Since 1998, he has worked mainly with acceptance and commitment therapy (ACT), both in his own practice and as a teacher and clinical supervisor. His clinical experience ranges from psychiatric disorders such as schizophrenia to common anxiety and mood disorders with high prevalence in the general population.

Foreword writer **Steven C. Hayes, PhD,** is Nevada Foundation Professor and director of clinical training in the department of psychology at the University of Nevada. An author of forty-one books and nearly 600 scientific articles, his career has focused on analysis of the nature of human language and cognition, and its application to the understanding and alleviation of human suffering and promotion of human prosperity. Among other associations, Hayes has been president of the Association for Behavioral and Cognitive Therapies, and the Association for Contextual Behavioral Science. His work has received several awards, including the Impact of Science on Application Award from the Society for the Advancement of Behavior Analysis, and the Lifetime Achievement Award from the Association for Behavioral and Cognitive Therapies.

Index

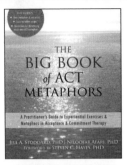
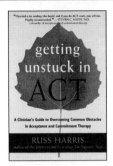

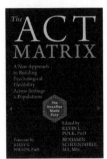

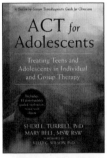